The Cumberbatch Tele-Accessibility Index related to Oklahoma and its seven neighboring states, i.e. Texas, Louisiana, Colorado, Arkansas, etc Years - 1996 - 2006!

The information was obtained from The U.S. Census Bureau, and the Federal Communications Commission (FCC) of The United States of America.

Table of Contents

Executive Summary

The conclusion of this research paper is that there does exist a positive correlation between the level of tele-accessibility and the rate of income per household, which was experienced between the states of Oklahoma, Colorado, Kansas, Missouri, Texas, Louisiana, Arkansas, and New Mexico, for the time period between 1996-2006.

Definitions

To obtain a better understanding of the paper I will provide definitions of various words which will be used throughout the document at the beginning, and are stated below.

The term **Fixed Lines** is a phrase which is used to describe the number of land-line or telephone lines that an individual has in their home, office, place of business, or in various other locations.

The term **Mobile Lines** is a phrase which is used to describe the number of mobile or cellular (cell) phones that an individual has, which may be used for personal, business or for numerous other purposes.

The term **Tele-Accessibility** is a phrase which is used to describe the total number of fixed plus mobile lines for a given year, which is then divided by the number of the population for that same time period. For example if a state has a tele-accessibility level of 1.7618, this means that the average household has access to 1.7618 means of communicating, i.e. a fixed and mobile telephone line, a fixed line, a mobile line, or some variation of these two terms.

The term **Income per Household/10,000** is a phrase which I created so that one could more easily compare the average income per household with the level of tele-accessibility experienced at that point in time. For the tele-accessibility numbers are relatively small and therefore to compare this variable with the income per household without making their sizes relatively similar in magnitude would be challenging, and thus may minimize or diminish the over-all effect of the paper.

The term **Correlation Coefficient** is a phrase which is used to describe the extent to which two independent variables i.e. income per household and tele-accessibility move in a similar direction when compared with each other. Therefore if they are positively correlated then one would expect that as the level of tele-accessibility increases or rises in a specific year, one would also be able to observe the level of income per household also becoming greater or larger, for that time period as well.

The level of Tele-Accessibility in the year 1996

In the year 1996 the level of access to telecommunications i.e. the tele-accessibility rate in the state of Oklahoma was equal to 0.55411, a measurement which was rounded off to five decimal places. This means that on average 55.411% of the residents of Oklahoma at that time period had access to various forms of telecommunication devices, i.e. fixed and mobile phone line services. This number does not adequately reflect the total number of tele-accessibility for the state of Oklahoma at that time period for it only provides information in relation to the number of fixed line subscribers. This is due to the fact that for the years 1996-1998 there were no reporting requirements placed upon the various cellular service providers, though they did provide some aggregate statistics this information is not represented on an individual state level. The level of income per household for that same time period was equal to **$31,357.00**. The correlation coefficient measurement for these two variables is equal to **0.90488** (rounded to 5 decimal places), this means that **90.488%** of the reason for which one variable moves in a specific direction can be explained by the variation in the other variable i.e. based upon the statistics provided **90.488%** of the variation in the level of income per household in the state of Oklahoma at that time period could be explained by the variation in the level of tele-accessibility, or access to telecommunications.

The state of Colorado had the highest level of tele-accessibility for the year 1996, at a rate of 0.62454, a measurement which was rounded off to five decimal places. This means that on average 62.454% of the residents of Colorado at that time period had access to various forms of telecommunication devices, i.e. fixed and mobile phone line services. This number does not adequately reflect the total number of tele-accessibility for the state of Colorado at that time period for it only provides information in relation to the number of fixed line subscribers. This is due to the fact that for the years 1996-1998 there were no reporting requirements placed upon the various cellular service providers, though they did provide some aggregate statistics this information is not represented on an individual state level. The level of income per household for that same time period was equal to **$44,349.00**. The correlation coefficient measurement for these two variables is equal to **0.90488** (rounded to 5 decimal places), this means that **90.488%** of the reason for which one variable moves in a specific direction can be explained by the variation in the other variable i.e. based upon the statistics provided **90.488%** of the variation in the level of income per household in the state of Colorado at that time period could be explained by the variation in the level of tele-accessibility, or access to telecommunications.

The state of Kansas had the second highest level of tele-accessibility for the year 1996, at a rate of 0.57203, a measurement which was rounded off to five decimal places. This means that on average 57.203% of the residents of Kansas at that time period had access to various forms of telecommunication devices, i.e. fixed and mobile phone line services. This number does not adequately reflect the total number of tele-accessibility for the state of Kansas at that time period for it only provides information in relation to the number of fixed line subscribers. This is due to the fact that for the years 1996-1998 there were no reporting requirements placed upon the various cellular service providers, though they did provide some aggregate statistics this information is not represented on an individual state level. The level of income per household for that same time period was equal to **$35,867.00**. The correlation coefficient measurement for these two variables is equal to **0.90488** (rounded to 5 decimal places), this means that **90.488%** of the reason for which one variable moves in a specific direction can be explained by the variation in the other variable i.e. based upon the statistics provided **90.488%** of the variation in the level of income per household in the state of Kansas at that time period could be explained by the variation in the level of tele-accessibility, or access to telecommunications.

The state of New Mexico had the lowest level of tele-accessibility for the year 1996, at a rate of 0.47719, a measurement which was rounded off to five decimal places. This means that on average 47.719% of the residents of New Mexico at that time period had access to various forms of telecommunication devices, i.e. fixed and mobile phone line services. This number does not adequately reflect the total number of tele-accessibility for the state of New Mexico at that time period for it only provides information in relation to the number of fixed line subscribers. This is due to the fact that for the years 1996-1998 there were no reporting requirements placed upon the various cellular service providers, though they did provide some aggregate statistics this information is not represented on an individual state level. The level of income per household for that same time period was equal to **$29,386.00**. The correlation coefficient measurement for these two variables is equal to **0.90488** (rounded to 5 decimal places), this means that **90.488%** of the reason for which one variable moves in a specific direction can be explained by the variation in the other variable i.e. based upon the statistics provided **90.488%** of the variation in the level of income per household in the state of New Mexico at that time period could be explained by the variation in the level of tele-accessibility, or access to telecommunications.

The level of Tele-Accessibility in the year 1999

In the year 1999 the level of access to telecommunications i.e. the tele-accessibility rate in the state of Oklahoma was equal to 0.86727, a measurement which was rounded off to five decimal places. This means that on average 86.727% of the residents of Oklahoma at that time period had access to various forms of telecommunication devices, i.e. fixed and mobile phone line services. The level of income per household for that same time period was equal to **$33,311.00**. The correlation coefficient measurement for these two variables is equal to **0.87354** (rounded to 5 decimal places), this means that **87.354%** of the reason for which one variable moves in a specific direction can be explained by the variation in the other variable i.e. based upon the statistics provided **87.354%** of the variation in the level of income per household in the state of Oklahoma at that time period could be explained by the variation in the level of tele-accessibility, or access to telecommunications.

The state of Colorado had the highest level of tele-accessibility for the year 1999, at a rate of 1.08894, a measurement which was rounded off to five decimal places. This means that on average 108.894% of the residents of Colorado at that time period had access to various forms of telecommunication devices, i.e. fixed and mobile phone line services. The level of income per household for that same time period was equal to

$46,950.00. The correlation coefficient measurement for these two variables is equal to **0.87354** (rounded to 5 decimal places), this means that **87.354%** of the reason for which one variable moves in a specific direction can be explained by the variation in the other variable i.e. based upon the statistics provided **87.354%** of the variation in the level of income per household in the state of Colorado at that time period could be explained by the variation in the level of tele-accessibility, or access to telecommunications.

The state of Missouri had the second highest level of tele-accessibility for the year 1999, at a rate of 1.00252, a measurement which was rounded off to five decimal places. This means that on average 100.252% of the residents of Missouri at that time period had access to various forms of telecommunication devices, i.e. fixed and mobile phone line services. The level of income per household for that same time period was equal to **$40,166.00**. The correlation coefficient measurement for these two variables is equal to **0.87354** (rounded to 5 decimal places), this means that **87.354%** of the reason for which one variable moves in a specific direction can be explained by the variation in the other variable i.e. based upon the statistics provided **87.354%** of the variation in the level of income per household in the state of Missouri at that time period could be explained by the variation in the level of tele-accessibility, or access to telecommunications.

The state of New Mexico had the lowest level of tele-accessibility for the year 1999, at a rate of 0.75772, a measurement which was rounded off to five decimal places. This means that on average 75.772% of the residents of New Mexico at that time period had access to various forms of telecommunication devices, i.e. fixed and mobile phone line services. The level of income per household for that same time period was equal to **$31,981.00**. The correlation coefficient measurement for these two variables is equal to **0.87354** (rounded to 5 decimal places), this means that **87.354%** of the reason for which one variable moves in a specific direction can be explained by the variation in the other variable i.e. based upon the statistics provided **87.354%** of the variation in the level of income per household in the state of New Mexico at that time period could be explained by the variation in the level of tele-accessibility, or access to telecommunications.

The level of Tele-Accessibility in the year 2001

In the year 2001 the level of access to telecommunications i.e. the tele-accessibility rate in the state of Oklahoma was equal to 0.9594, a measurement which was rounded off to five decimal places. This means that on average 95.94% of the residents of Oklahoma at that time period had access to various forms of telecommunication devices, i.e. fixed and mobile phone line services. The level of income per household for that same time period was equal to **$33,311.00**. The correlation coefficient measurement for these two variables is equal to **0.87354** (rounded to 5 decimal places), this means that **87.354%** of the reason for which one variable moves in a specific direction can be explained by the variation in the other variable i.e. based upon the statistics provided **87.354%** of the variation in the level of income per household in the state of Oklahoma at that time period could be explained by the variation in the level of tele-accessibility, or access to telecommunications.

The state of Colorado had the highest level of tele-accessibility for the year 2001, at a rate of 1.14891 a measurement which was rounded off to five decimal places. This means that on average 114.891% of the residents of Colorado at that time period had access to various forms of telecommunication devices, i.e. fixed and mobile phone line services. The level of income per household for that same time period was equal to **$ 50,053.00**.

The correlation coefficient measurement for these two variables is equal to **0.83569** (rounded to 5 decimal places), this means that **83.569%** of the reason for which one variable moves in a specific direction can be explained by the variation in the other variable i.e. based upon the statistics provided **83.569%** of the variation in the level of income per household in the state of Colorado at that time period could be explained by the variation in the level of tele-accessibility, or access to telecommunications.

The state of Texas had the second highest level of tele-accessibility for the year 2001, at a rate of 1.04722, a measurement which was rounded off to five decimal places. This means that on average 104.722% of the residents of Texas at that time period had access to various forms of telecommunication devices, i.e. fixed and mobile phone line services. The level of income per household for that same time period was equal to **$40,547.00**. The correlation coefficient measurement for these two variables is equal to **0.83569** (rounded to 5 decimal places), this means that **83.569%** of the reason for which one variable moves in a specific direction can be explained by the variation in the other variable i.e. based upon the statistics provided **83.569%** of the variation in the level of income per household in the state of Texas at that time period could be explained by the variation in the level of tele-accessibility, or access to telecommunications.

The state of New Mexico had the lowest level of tele-accessibility for the year 2001, at a rate of 0.91023, a measurement which was rounded off to five decimal places. This means that on average 91.023% of the residents of New Mexico at that time period had access to various forms of telecommunication devices, i.e. fixed and mobile phone line services. The level of income per household for that same time period was equal to **$34,599.00**. The correlation coefficient measurement for these two variables is equal to **0.83569** (rounded to 5 decimal places), this means that **83.569%** of the reason for which one variable moves in a specific direction can be explained by the variation in the other variable i.e. based upon the statistics provided **83.569%** of the variation in the level of income per household in the state of New Mexico at that time period could be explained by the variation in the level of tele-accessibility, or access to telecommunications.

The level of Tele-Accessibility in the year 2003

In the year 2003 the level of access to telecommunications i.e. the tele-accessibility rate in the state of Oklahoma was equal to 0.98316, a measurement which was rounded off to five decimal places. This means that on average 98.316% of the residents of Oklahoma at that time period had access to various forms of telecommunication devices, i.e. fixed and mobile phone line services. The level of income per household for that same time period was equal to **$36,733.00**. The correlation coefficient measurement for these two variables is equal to **0.66783** (rounded to 5 decimal places), this means that **66.783%** of the reason for which one variable moves in a specific direction can be explained by the variation in the other variable i.e. based upon the statistics provided **66.783%** of the variation in the level of income per household in the state of Oklahoma at that time period could be explained by the variation in the level of tele-accessibility, or access to telecommunications.

The state of Colorado had the highest level of tele-accessibility for the year 2003, at a rate of 1.15507 a measurement which was rounded off to five decimal places. This means that on average 115.507% of the residents of Colorado at that time period had access to various forms of telecommunication devices, i.e. fixed and mobile phone line services. The level of income per household for that same time period was equal to **$50,224.00**.

The correlation coefficient measurement for these two variables is equal to **0.66783** (rounded to 5 decimal places), this means that **66.783%** of the reason for which one variable moves in a specific direction can be explained by the variation in the other variable i.e. based upon the statistics provided **66.783%** of the variation in the level of income per household in the state of Colorado at that time period could be explained by the variation in the level of tele-accessibility, or access to telecommunications.

The state of Louisiana had the second highest level of tele-accessibility for the year 2003, at a rate of 1.08594, a measurement which was rounded off to five decimal places. This means that on average 108.594% of the residents of Louisiana at that time period had access to various forms of telecommunication devices, i.e. fixed and mobile phone line services. The level of income per household for that same time period was equal to **$34,307.00**. The correlation coefficient measurement for these two variables is equal to **0.66783** (rounded to 5 decimal places), this means that **66.783%** of the reason for which one variable moves in a specific direction can be explained by the variation in the other variable i.e. based upon the statistics provided **66.783%** of the variation in the level of income per household in the state of Louisiana at that time period could be explained by the variation in the level of tele-accessibility, or access to telecommunications.

The state of New Mexico had the lowest level of tele-accessibility for the year 2003, at a rate of 0.97668, a measurement which was rounded off to five decimal places. This means that on average 97.668% of the residents of New Mexico at that time period had access to various forms of telecommunication devices, i.e. fixed and mobile phone line services. The level of income per household for that same time period was equal to **$35,265.00**. The correlation coefficient measurement for these two variables is equal to **0.66783** (rounded to 5 decimal places), this means that **66.783%** of the reason for which one variable moves in a specific direction can be explained by the variation in the other variable i.e. based upon the statistics provided **66.783%** of the variation in the level of income per household in the state of New Mexico at that time period could be explained by the variation in the level of tele-accessibility, or access to telecommunications.

The level of Tele-Accessibility in the year 2006

In the year 2006 the level of access to telecommunications i.e. the tele-accessibility rate in the state of Oklahoma was equal to 1.12252, a measurement which was rounded off to five decimal places. This means that on average 112.252% of the residents of Oklahoma at that time period had access to various forms of telecommunication devices, i.e. fixed and mobile phone line services. The level of income per household for that same time period was equal to **$38,191.00**. The correlation coefficient measurement for these two variables is equal to **0.38977** (rounded to 5 decimal places), this means that **38.977%** of the reason for which one variable moves in a specific direction can be explained by the variation in the other variable i.e. based upon the statistics provided **38.977%** of the variation in the level of income per household in the state of Oklahoma at that time period could be explained by the variation in the level of tele-accessibility, or access to telecommunications. The state of Oklahoma had the lowest level of tele-accessibility for any of the eight states which are being analyzed for the year of 2006.

The state of Louisiana had the highest level of tele-accessibility for the year 2006, at a rate of 1.27184 a measurement which was rounded off to five decimal places. This means that on average 127.184% of the residents of Louisiana at that time period had access to various forms of telecommunication devices, i.e. fixed and mobile phone line services.

The level of income per household for that same time period was equal to **$37,740.00**. The correlation coefficient measurement for these two variables is equal to **0.38977** (rounded to 5 decimal places), this means that **38.977%** of the reason for which one variable moves in a specific direction can be explained by the variation in the other variable i.e. based upon the statistics provided **38.977%** of the variation in the level of income per household in the state of Louisiana at that time period could be explained by the variation in the level of tele-accessibility, or access to telecommunications.

The state of Missouri had the second highest level of tele-accessibility for the year 2006, at a rate of 1.24188, a measurement which was rounded off to five decimal places. This means that on average 124.188% of the residents of Missouri at that time period had access to various forms of telecommunication devices, i.e. fixed and mobile phone line services. The level of income per household for that same time period was equal to **$43,310.00**. The correlation coefficient measurement for these two variables is equal to **0.38977** (rounded to 5 decimal places), this means that **38.977%** of the reason for which one variable moves in a specific direction can be explained by the variation in the other variable i.e. based upon the statistics provided **38.977%** of the variation in the level of income per household in the state of Missouri at that time period could be explained by the variation in the level of tele-accessibility, or access to telecommunications.

The level of Tele-Accessibility in the State of Oklahoma for the years 1996-2006

For the state of Oklahoma if one looks at the bar charts which represent the changes in the rate of tele-accessibility and income per household over the time period of 1996-2006, you are able to see that both variables move in the same direction, and thus are positively correlated. The correlation that exists between these two variables for the same time period is equal to a rate of 0.93323 a measurement which was rounded off to five decimal places, or states that 93.323% of the variation in the level of income per household in the state of Oklahoma may be explained by its access to telecommunications.

The level of Tele-Accessibility in the State of Arkansas for the years 1996-2006

For the state of Arkansas if one looks at the bar charts which represent the changes in the rate of tele-accessibility and income per household over the time period of 1996-2006, you are able to see that both variables move in the same direction, and thus are positively correlated. The correlation that exists between these two variables for the same time period is equal to a rate of 0.93131 a measurement which was rounded off to five decimal places, or states that 93.131% of the variation in the level of income per household in the state of Arkansas may be explained by its access to telecommunications.

The level of Tele-Accessibility in the State of Colorado for the years 1996-2006

For the state of Colorado if one looks at the bar charts which represent the changes in the rate of tele-accessibility and income per household over the time period of 1996-2006, you are able to see that both variables move in the same direction, and thus are positively correlated. The correlation that exists between these two variables for the same time period is equal to a rate of **0.69569** a measurement which was rounded off to five decimal places, or states that **69.569%** of the variation in the level of income per household in the state of Colorado may be explained by its access to telecommunications.

The level of Tele-Accessibility in the State of Kansas for the years 1996-2006

For the state of Kansas if one looks at the bar charts which represent the changes in the rate of tele-accessibility and income per household over the time period of 1996-2006, you are able to see that both variables move in the same direction, and thus are positively correlated. The correlation that exists between these two variables for the same time period is equal to a rate of **0.82373** a measurement which was rounded off to five decimal places, or states that **82.373%** of the variation in the level of income per household in the state of Kansas may be explained by its access to telecommunications.

The level of Tele-Accessibility in the State of Louisiana for the years 1996-2006

For the state of Louisiana if one looks at the bar charts which represent the changes in the rate of tele-accessibility and income per household over the time period of 1996-2006, you are able to see that both variables move in the same direction, and thus are positively correlated. The correlation that exists between these two variables for the same time period is equal to a rate of 0.71918 a measurement which was rounded off to five decimal places, or states that 71.918% of the variation in the level of income per household in the state of Louisiana may be explained by its access to telecommunications.

The level of Tele-Accessibility in the State of Missouri for the years 1996-2006

For the state of Missouri if one looks at the bar charts which represent the changes in the rate of tele-accessibility and income per household over the time period of 1996-2006, you are able to see that both variables move in the same direction, and thus are positively correlated. The correlation that exists between these two variables for the same time period is equal to a rate of 0.62252 a measurement which was rounded off to five decimal places, or states that 62.252% of the variation in the level of income per household in the state of Missouri may be explained by its access to telecommunications.

The level of Tele-Accessibility in the State of New Mexico for the years 1996-2006

For the state of New Mexico if one looks at the bar charts which represent the changes in the rate of tele-accessibility and income per household over the time period of 1996-2006, you are able to see that both variables move in the same direction, and thus are positively correlated. The correlation that exists between these two variables for the same time period is equal to a rate of 0.95708 a measurement which was rounded off to five decimal places, or states that 95.708% of the variation in the level of income per household in the state of New Mexico may be explained by its access to telecommunications.

The level of Tele-Accessibility in the State of Texas for the years 1996-2006

For the state of Texas if one looks at the bar charts which represent the changes in the rate of tele-accessibility and income per household over the time period of 1996-2006, you are able to see that both variables move in the same direction, and thus are positively correlated. The correlation that exists between these two variables for the same time period is equal to a rate of 0.91767 a measurement which was rounded off to five decimal places, or states that 91.767% of the variation in the level of income per household in the state of Texas may be explained by its access to telecommunications.

Conclusion

For the states which are represented in this study one is able to observe by taking a look at the bar charts which represent the changes in the rate of tele-accessibility and income per household over the time period of 1996-2006, that both variables move in the same direction, and thus are positively correlated. The correlation that exists between these two variables for the same time period range from a rate of 0.62252 to 0.95708, a measurement which was rounded off to five decimal places, or states that between 62.252% and 95.708% of the variation in the level of income per households in the various states may be explained by its access to telecommunications.

One observation which I have noticed is that once the level of tele-accessibility reaches a rate of 1.0 or higher, the strength of the correlation factor between the two variables are diminished or reduced. This means that there are other variables which play a larger contributing role to the continued growth in income per household than the tele-accessibility measurement, beyond this point.

Appendix

1. The excel spreadsheets and bar charts which show the numbers from which the conclusions were derived.

	State	Population	Number of Fixed Lines	Number of Mobile Lines	Tele - Accessibility (Fixed + Mobile lines /Population)	Income per Household	Income per Household / 10,000
				Year - 1996			
1	Colorado	3812716	2,381,182	N/A	0.624536944	$ 44,349.00	$ 4.43
2	Kansas	2598266	1,486,306	N/A	0.572037659	$ 35,867.00	$ 3.59
3	Missouri	5367888	3,064,182	N/A	0.570835681	$ 37,640.00	$ 3.76
4	Texas	19006240	10,678,438	N/A	0.561838533	$ 35,254.00	$ 3.53
5	Oklahoma	3289634	1,822,825	N/A	0.554111795	$ 31,357.00	$ 3.14
6	Louisiana	4338763	2,265,803	N/A	0.52222327	$ 32,317.00	$ 3.23
7	Arkansas	2504858	1,288,457	N/A	0.51438325	$ 27,471.00	$ 2.75
8	New Mexico	1706151	814,166	N/A	0.477194574	$ 29,386.00	$ 2.94

Correlation Coefficient - 0.9048815

Note:
In the years 1996-98 no reporting requirements were placed upon the cellular industry, thus limited information is available.

Websites used:

http://www.census.gov/hhes/www/income/income98.html
http://www.fcc.gov/Bureaus/Common_Carrier/Reports/FCC-State_Link/IAD/trend801.pdf

	Year - 1996		
	State	**Tele - Accessibility**	**Income per Household / 10000**
1	Colorado	0.62454	4.43
2	Kansas	0.57203	3.59
3	Missouri	0.57084	3.76
4	Texas	0.56184	3.53
5	Oklahoma	0.55411	3.14
6	Louisiana	0.52222	3.23
7	Arkansas	0.51438	2.75
8	New Mexico	0.47719	2.94

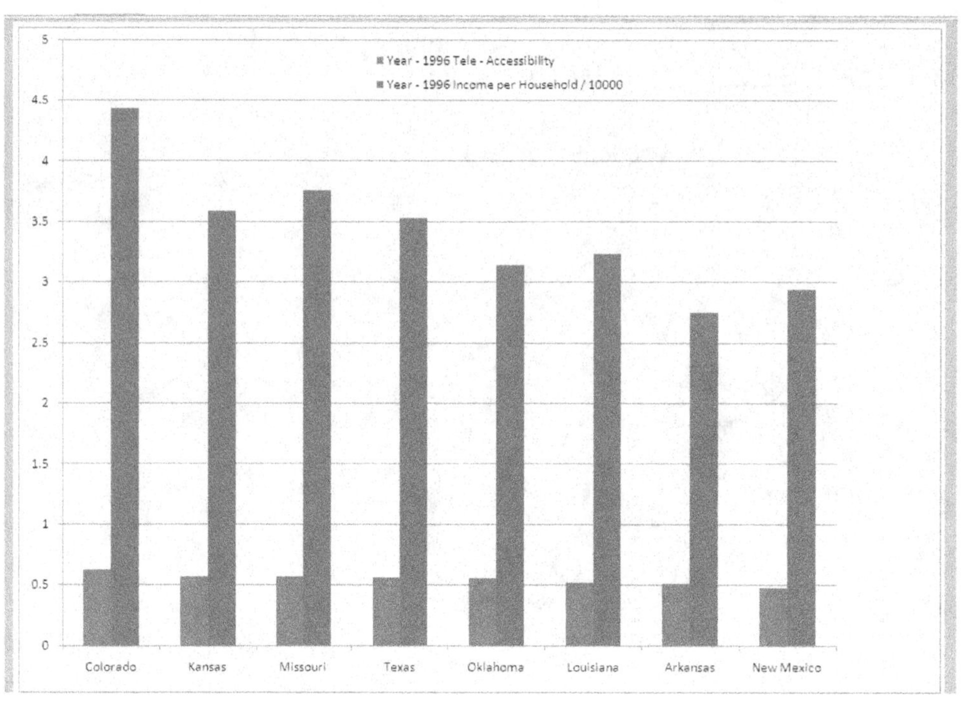
Year - 1996 Tele - Accessibility
Year - 1996 Income per Household / 10000
5
4.5
4
3.5
3
2.5
2
1.5
1
0.5
0
Colorado
Kansas
Missouri
Texas
Oklahoma
Louisiana
Arkansas
New Mexico

	State	Population	Number of Fixed Lines	Number of Mobile Lines	Tele - Accessibility (Fixed + Mobile lines /Population)	Income per Household	Income per Household / 10,000
				Year - 1997			
1	Colorado	3891293	2,643,505	N/A	0.679338462	$ 44,349.00	$ 4.43
2	Texas	19355427	12,006,252	N/A	0.620304166	$ 35,254.00	$ 3.53
3	Missouri	5407113	3,324,016	N/A	0.614748758	$ 37,640.00	$ 3.76
4	Kansas	2616339	1,584,824	N/A	0.605741076	$ 35,867.00	$ 3.59
5	Oklahoma	3314259	1,954,375	N/A	0.589686865	$ 31,357.00	$ 3.14
6	Louisiana	4351390	2,435,338	N/A	0.559668979	$ 32,317.00	$ 3.23
7	Arkansas	2524007	1,368,534	N/A	0.542206896	$ 27,471.00	$ 2.75
8	New Mexico	1722939	901,359	N/A	0.523152009	$ 29,386.00	$ 2.94

Correlation Coefficient - 0.941487

Note:
In the years 1996-98 no reporting requirements were placed upon the cellular industry, thus limited information is available.

Websites used:

http://www.census.gov/hhes/www/income/income98.html
http://www.fcc.gov/Bureaus/Common_Carrier/Reports/FCC-State_Link/IAD/trend801.pdf

	Year - 1997		
	State	**Tele - Accessibility**	**Income per Household / 10000**
1	Colorado	0.67934	4.43
2	Texas	0.6203	3.53
3	Missouri	0.61475	3.76
4	Kansas	0.60574	3.59
5	Oklahoma	0.58968	3.14
6	Louisiana	0.55967	3.23
7	Arkansas	0.54220	2.75
8	New Mexico	0.52315	2.94

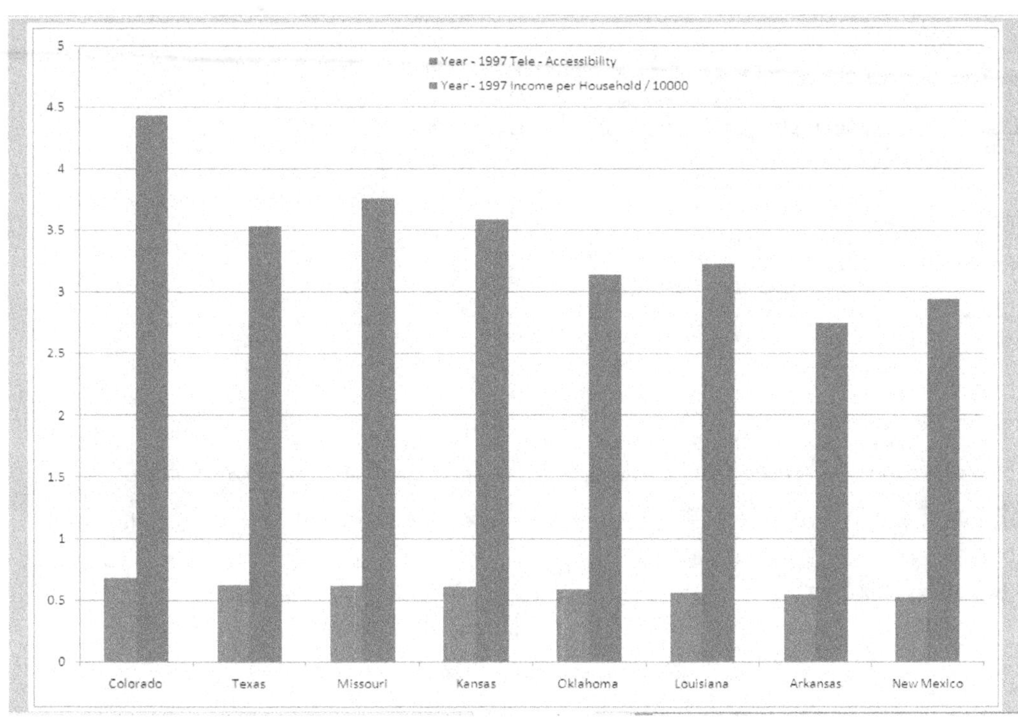
Year - 1997 Tele - Accessibility
Year - 1997 Income per Household / 10000
5
4.5
4
3.5
3
2.5
2
1.5
1
0.5
0
Colorado
Texas
Missouri
Kansas
Oklahoma
Louisiana
Arkansas
New Mexico

	State	Population	Number of Fixed Lines	Number of Mobile Lines	Tele - Accessibility (Fixed + Mobile lines /Population)	Income per Household	Income per Household / 10,000
				Year - 1998			
1	Colorado	3968967	2,756,829	N/A	0.6945961	$ 44,349.00	$ 4.43
2	Texas	19712389	12,616,588	N/A	0.640033433	$ 35,254.00	$ 3.53
3	Missouri	5437562	3,450,562	N/A	0.634578879	$ 37,640.00	$ 3.76
4	Kansas	2638667	1,649,694	N/A	0.625199769	$ 35,867.00	$ 3.59
5	Oklahoma	3339478	2,018,166	N/A	0.604335767	$ 31,357.00	$ 3.14
6	Louisiana	4362758	2,529,434	N/A	0.579778663	$ 32,317.00	$ 3.23
7	Arkansas	2538202	1,422,174	N/A	0.560307651	$ 27,471.00	$ 2.75
8	New Mexico	1733535	925,007	N/A	0.533595803	$ 29,386.00	$ 2.94

Correlation Coefficient - 0.934894

Note:
In the years 1996-98 no reporting requirements were placed upon the cellular industry, thus limited information is available.

Websites used:

http://www.census.gov/hhes/www/income/income98.html
http://www.fcc.gov/Bureaus/Common_Carrier/Reports/FCC-State_Link/IAD/trend801.pdf

	State	Year - 1998 Tele - Accessibility	Income per Household / 10000
1	Colorado	0.69459	4.43
2	Texas	0.64003	3.53
3	Missouri	0.63458	3.76
4	Kansas	0.62519	3.59
5	Oklahoma	0.60434	3.14
6	Louisiana	0.57978	3.23
7	Arkansas	0.56031	2.75
8	New Mexico	0.53359	2.94

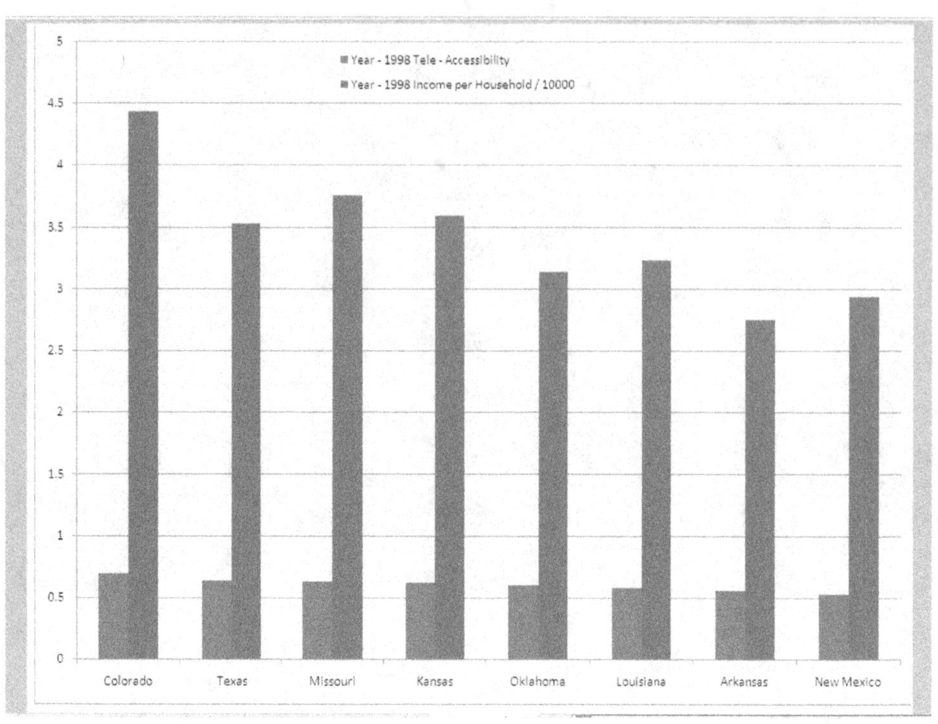
Year - 1998 Tele - Accessibility
Year - 1998 Income per Household / 10000
5
4.5
4
3.5
3
2.5
2
1.5
1
0.5
0
Colorado
Texas
Missouri
Kansas
Oklahoma
Louisiana
Arkansas
New Mexico

	State	Population	Number of Fixed Lines	Number of Mobile Lines	Tele - Accessibility (Fixed + Mobile lines /Population)	Income per Household	Income per Household / 10,000
				Year - 1999			
1	Colorado	4056133	2,864,170	1,552,718	1.088940624	$ 46,950.00	$ 4.70
2	Missouri	5468338	3,626,683	1,855,452	1.00252307	$ 40,166.00	$ 4.02
3	Texas	20044141	13,174,403	5,792,453	0.946254369	$ 37,320.00	$ 3.73
4	Kansas	2654052	1,720,106	669,472	0.90035086	$ 37,618.00	$ 3.76
5	Louisiana	4372035	2,585,779	1,227,106	0.872107611	$ 33,218.00	$ 3.32
6	Arkansas	2551373	1,501,281	719,919	0.870590071	$ 28,398.00	$ 2.84
7	Oklahoma	3358044	2,085,686	826,637	0.867267671	$ 33,311.00	$ 3.33
8	New Mexico	1739844	954,496	363,827	0.757724831	$ 31,981.00	$ 3.20

Correlation Coefficient - 0.873539

Websites used:

http://www.census.gov/hhes/www/income/income98.html
http://www.fcc.gov/Bureaus/Common_Carrier/Reports/FCC-State_Link/IAD/trend801.pdf

		Year - 1999	
	State	**Tele - Accessibility**	**Income per Household / 10000**
1	Colorado	1.08894	4.70
2	Missouri	1.00252	4.02
3	Texas	0.94635	3.73
4	Kansas	0.90035	3.76
5	Louisiana	0.87211	3.32
6	Arkansas	0.87059	2.84
7	Oklahoma	0.86727	3.33
8	New Mexico	0.75772	3.20

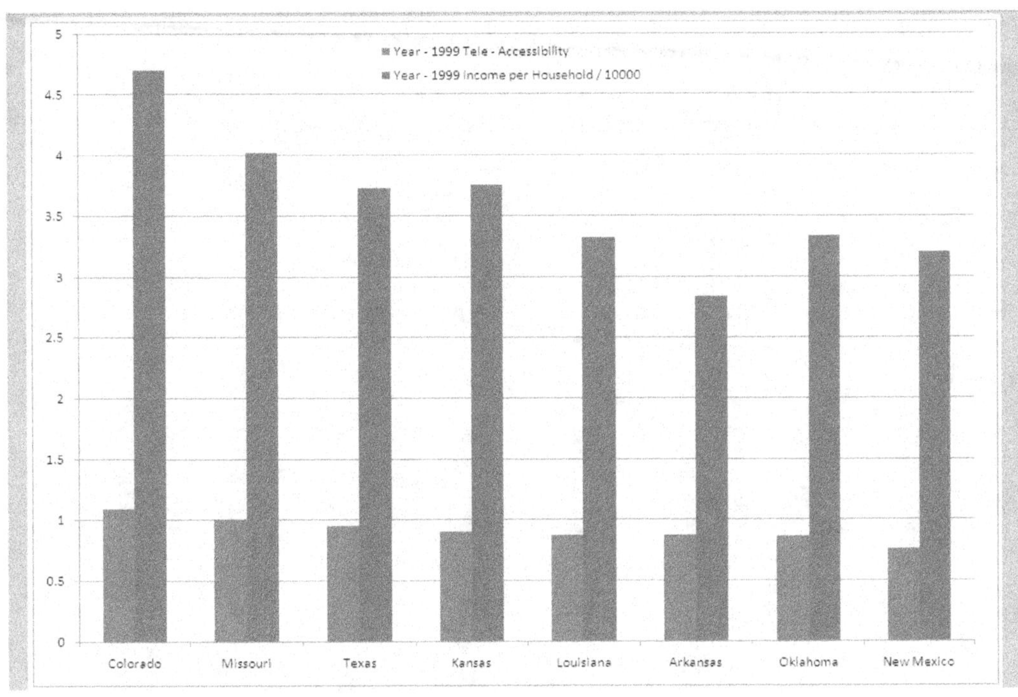
Year - 1999 Tele - Accessibility
Year - 1999 Income per Household / 10000
5
4.5
4
3.5
3
2.5
2
1.5
1
0.5
0
Colorado
Missouri
Texas
Kansas
Louisiana
Arkansas
Oklahoma
New Mexico

	Year - 2000							
	State	**Population**	**Number of Fixed Lines**	**Number of Mobile Lines**	**Tele - Accessibility (Fixed + Mobile lines /Population)**	**Income per Household**	**Income per Household / 10,000**	
1	Colorado	4,301,261	3,120,903	1,856,075	1.157097419	$48,506.00	$	4.85
2	Texas	20,851,820	13,750,684	7,489,180	1.018609599	$39,842.00	$	3.98
3	Missouri	5,595,211	3,688,948	1,767,411	0.975183778	$47,462.00	$	4.75
4	Kansas	2,688,418	1,740,944	801,293	0.945625643	$37,705.00	$	3.77
5	Arkansas	2,673,400	1,733,035	743,928	0.926521658	$30,293.00	$	3.03
6	Louisiana	4,468,976	2,796,882	1,306,457	0.918183271	$30,219.00	$	3.02
7	Oklahoma	3,450,654	1,739,301	1,124,214	0.829847038	$32,445.00	$	3.24
8	New Mexico	1,819,046	957,195	443,343	0.769929952	$35,254.00	$	3.53

Correlation Coefficient - 0.6981213

Websites used:

http://www.census.gov/hhes/www/income/income98.html
http://www.fcc.gov/Bureaus/Common_Carrier/Reports/FCC-State_Link/IAD/trend801.pdf

	Year - 2000		
	State	**Tele - Accessibility**	**Income per Household / 10000**
1	Colorado	1.15709	4.85
2	Texas	1.01861	3.98
3	Missouri	0.97518	4.75
4	Kansas	0.94562	3.77
5	Arkansas	0.92652	3.03
6	Louisiana	0.91818	3.02
7	Oklahoma	0.82984	3.24
8	New Mexico	0.76993	3.53

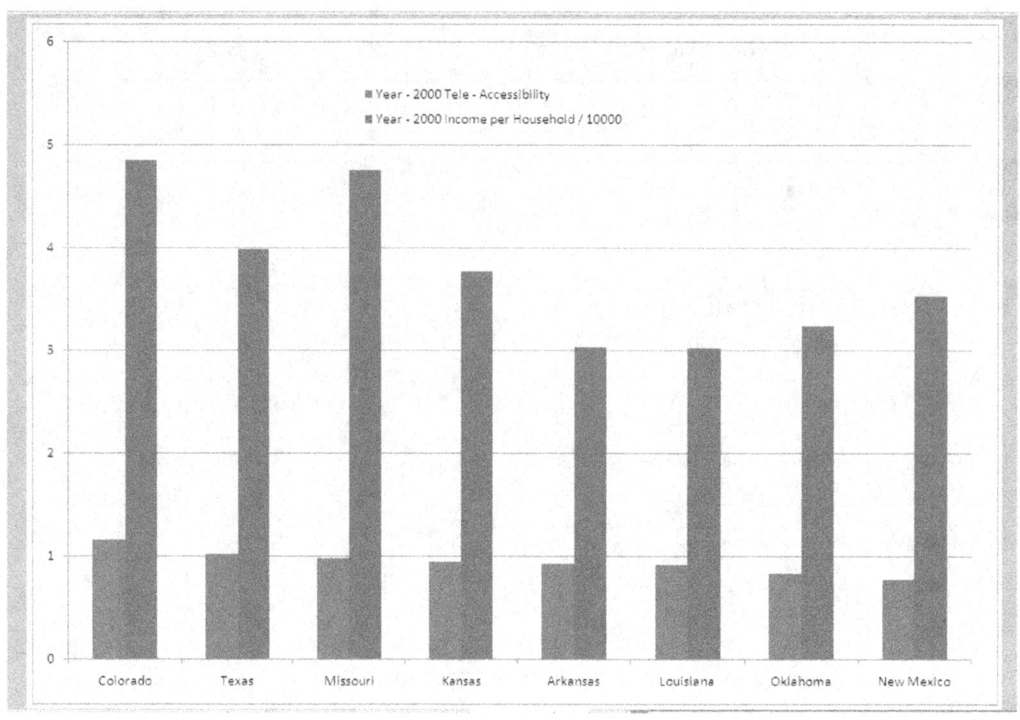
Year - 2000 Tele - Accessibility
Year - 2000 Income per Household / 10000
6
5
4
3
2
1
0
Colorado
Texas
Missouri
Kansas
Arkansas
Louisiana
Oklahoma
New Mexico

				Year - 2001			
	State	Population	Number of Fixed Lines	Number of Mobile Lines	Tele - Accessibility (Fixed + Mobile lines /Population)	Income per Household	Income per Household / 10,000
1	Colorado	4433997	2,948,466	2,145,816	1.148914174	$ 50,053.00	$ 5.01
2	Texas	21340494	13,192,061	9,156,187	1.047222618	$ 40,547.00	$ 4.05
3	Missouri	5641517	3,630,138	2,106,599	1.016878439	$ 43,884.00	$ 4.39
4	Louisiana	4460285	2,575,040	1,920,740	1.007958012	$ 33,194.00	$ 3.32
5	Kansas	2700979	1,666,630	956,050	0.971010882	$ 41,097.00	$ 4.11
6	Oklahoma	3464818	2,035,796	1,288,357	0.959401908	$ 34,554.00	$ 3.46
7	Arkansas	2,690,254	1,509,333	970,127	0.921645317	$ 31,798.00	$ 3.18
8	New Mexico	1829032	1,003,993	660,849	0.910231204	$ 34,599.00	$ 3.46

Correlation Coefficient - 0.835693

Websites used:

http://www.census.gov/hhes/www/income/income98.html
http://www.fcc.gov/Bureaus/Common_Carrier/Reports/FCC-State_Link/IAD/trend801.pdf

	State	Tele - Accessibility	Income per Household / 10000
		Year - 2001	
1	Colorado	1.14891	5.01
2	Texas	1.04722	4.05
3	Missouri	1.01688	4.39
4	Louisiana	1.00796	3.32
5	Kansas	0.97101	4.11
6	Oklahoma	0.95940	3.46
7	Arkansas	0.92165	3.18
8	New Mexico	0.91023	3.46

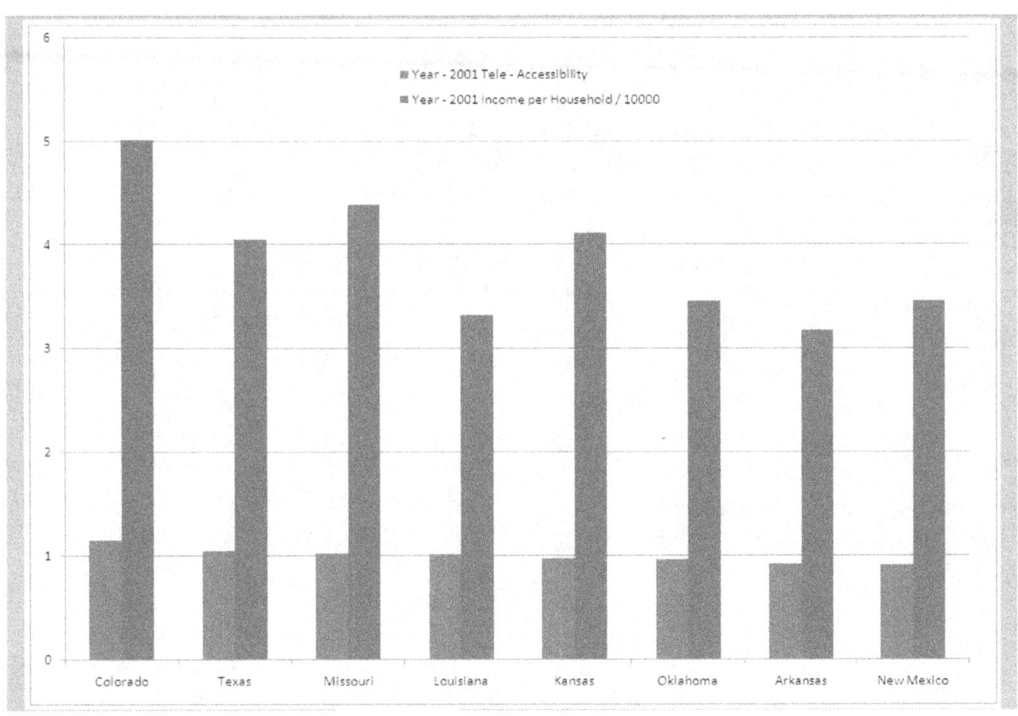

Year - 2001 Tele - Accessibility
Year - 2001 Income per Household / 10000
6
5
4
3
2
1
0
Colorado
Texas
Missouri
Louisiana
Kansas
Oklahoma
Arkansas
New Mexico

	State	Population	Number of Fixed Lines	Number of Mobile Lines	Tele - Accessibility (Fixed + Mobile lines /Population)	Income per Household	Income per Household / 10,000
				Year - 2002			
1	Colorado	4507762	3,124,180	2,358,748	1.21633041	$ 49,617.00	$ 4.96
2	Texas	21730350	12,949,056	10,133,280	1.062216485	$ 40,659.00	$ 4.07
3	Louisiana	4465490	2,542,272	2,190,613	1.059880327	$ 33,312.00	$ 3.33
4	Missouri	5676209	3,482,767	2,289,831	1.016981228	$ 43,955.00	$ 4.40
5	Oklahoma	3485515	1,934,157	1,440,970	0.968329501	$ 35,500.00	$ 3.55
6	Kansas	2712383	1,494,363	1,117,277	0.962858121	$ 42,523.00	$ 4.25
7	Arkansas	2,703,310	1,401,702	1,156,345	0.946264764	$ 32,423.00	$ 3.24
8	New Mexico	1850562	965,816	780,855	0.943859757	$ 35,251.00	$ 3.53

Correlation Coefficient - 0.686562831

Websites used:

http://www.census.gov/hhes/www/income/income98.html
http://www.fcc.gov/Bureaus/Common_Carrier/Reports/FCC-State_Link/IAD/trend801.pdf

		Year - 2002	
	State	**Tele - Accessibility**	**Income per Household / 10000**
1	Colorado	1.21633	4.96
2	Texas	1.06221	4.07
3	Louisiana	1.05988	3.33
4	Missouri	1.01698	4.40
5	Oklahoma	0.96833	3.55
6	Kansas	0.96286	4.25
7	Arkansas	0.94626	3.24
8	New Mexico	0.94386	3.53

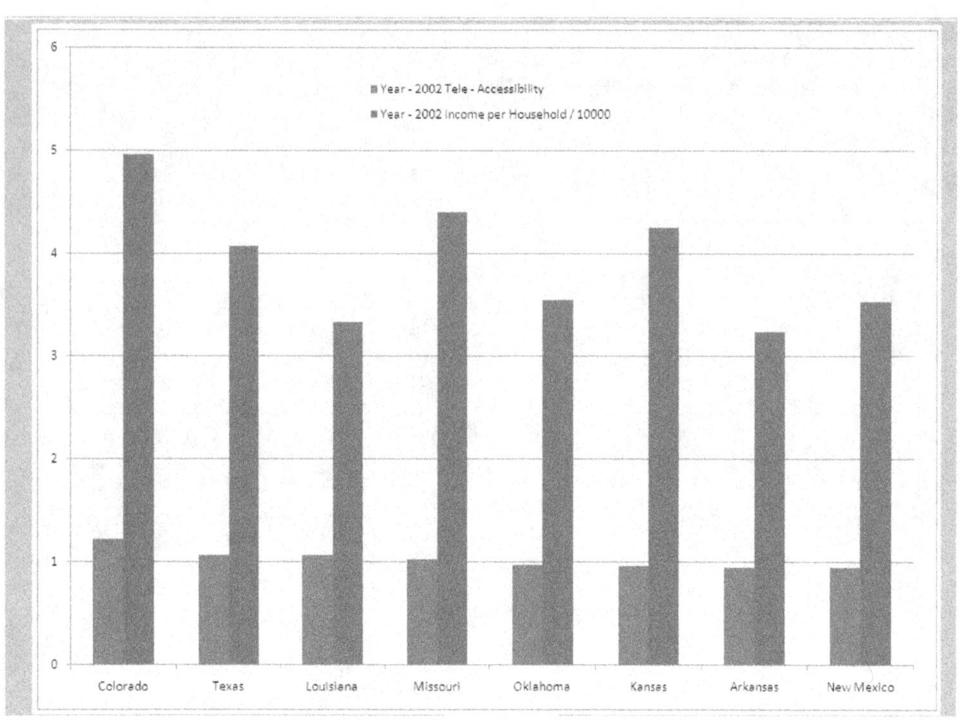
Year - 2002 Tele - Accessibility
Year - 2002 income per Household / 10000
6
5
4
3
2
1
0
Colorado
Texas
Louisiana
Missouri
Oklahoma
Kansas
Arkansas
New Mexico

	State	Population	Number of Fixed Lines	Number of Mobile Lines	Tele - Accessibility (Fixed + Mobile lines /Population)	Income per Household	Income per Household / 10,000
				Year - 2003			
1	Colorado	4555212	2,706,855	2,554,731	1.155069402	$50,224.00	$ 5.02
2	Louisiana	4473679	2,388,005	2,470,146	1.0859409	$34,307.00	$ 3.43
3	Missouri	5705971	3,386,695	2,691,255	1.065191183	$43,492.00	$ 4.35
4	Texas	22085973	12,039,565	11,327,700	1.058013835	$40,934.00	$ 4.09
5	Kansas	2721824	1,484,063	1,261,242	1.008626935	$43,622.00	$ 4.36
6	Arkansas	2720006	1,415,060	1,296,901	0.997042286	$33,259.00	$ 3.33
7	Oklahoma	3499937	1,826,796	1,614,191	0.98315684	$36,733.00	$ 3.67
8	New Mexico	1870113	967,109	859,408	0.97668804	$35,265.00	$ 3.53

Correlation Coefficient - 0.6678399

Websites used:

http://www.census.gov/hhes/www/income/income98.html
http://www.fcc.gov/Bureaus/Common_Carrier/Reports/FCC-State_Link/IAD/trend801.pdf

	State	Tele - Accessibility	Income per Household / 10000
		Year - 2003	
1	Colorado	1.15507	5.02
2	Louisiana	1.08594	3.43
3	Missouri	1.06519	4.35
4	Texas	1.05801	4.09
5	Kansas	1.00862	4.36
6	Arkansas	0.99704	3.33
7	Oklahoma	0.98316	3.67
8	New Mexico	0.97668	3.53

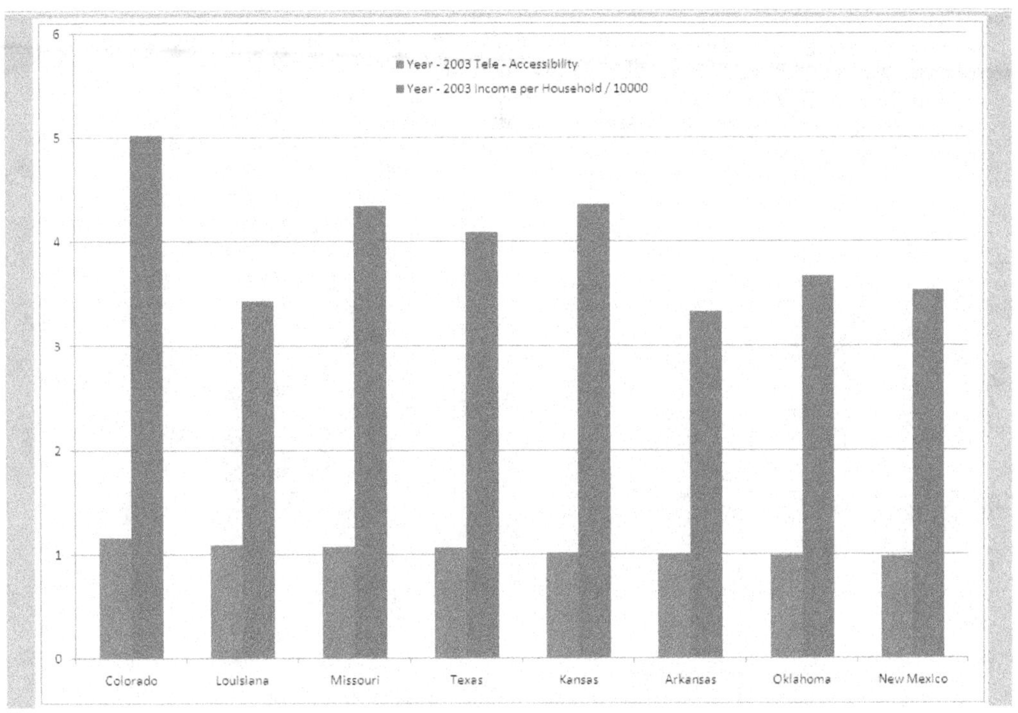
Year - 2003 Tele - Accessibility
Year - 2003 Income per Household / 10000
6
5
4
3
2
1
0
Colorado
Louisiana
Missouri
Texas
Kansas
Arkansas
Oklahoma
New Mexico

	State	Population	Number of Fixed Lines	Number of Mobile Lines	Tele - Accessibility (Fixed + Mobile lines /Population)	Income per Household	Income per Household / 10,000
				Year - 2004			
1	Colorado	4609264	2,606,817	2,808,195	1.174810555	$ 42,635.00	$ 4.26
2	Louisiana	4487966	2,268,720	2,834,716	1.137137848	$ 36,873.00	$ 3.69
3	Missouri	5744753	3,247,190	3,109,167	1.106463063	$ 38,637.00	$ 3.86
4	Texas	22454811	11,590,497	13,092,007	1.099207827	$ 38,200.00	$ 3.82
5	Kansas	2730828	1,380,166	1,454,087	1.037873129	$ 37,952.00	$ 3.80
6	Arkansas	2742898	1,371,860	1,458,673	1.031949784	$ 33,131.00	$ 3.31
7	New Mexico	1892182	940,052	987,813	1.018858123	$ 35,040.00	$ 3.50
8	Oklahoma	3516552	1,732,438	1,760,122	0.993177408	$ 34,503.00	$ 3.45

Correlation Coefficient - 0.815149877

Websites used:

http://www.census.gov/hhes/www/income/income98.html

http://www.fcc.gov/Bureaus/Common_Carrier/Reports/FCC-State_Link/IAD/trend801.pdf

	Year - 2004		
	State	**Tele - Accessibility**	**Income per Household / 10000**
1	Colorado	1.17481	4.26
2	Louisiana	1.13714	3.69
3	Missouri	1.10646	3.86
4	Texas	1.09921	3.82
5	Kansas	1.03787	3.80
6	Arkansas	1.03195	3.31
7	New Mexico	1.01886	3.50
8	Oklahoma	0.99317	3.45

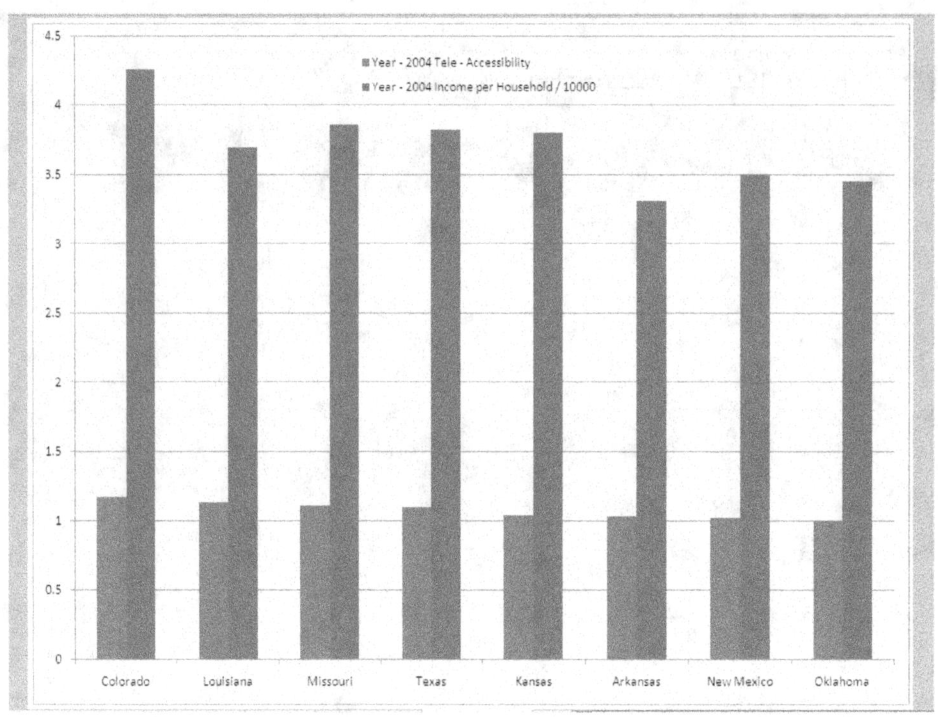

4.5
4
3.5
3
2.5
2
1.5
1
0.5
0
Year - 2004 Tele - Accessibility
Year - 2004 Income per Household / 10000
Colorado
Louisiana
Missouri
Texas
Kansas
Arkansas
New Mexico
Oklahoma

				Year - 2005			
	State	**Population**	**Number of Fixed Lines**	**Number of Mobile Lines**	**Tele - Accessibility (Fixed + Mobile lines /Population)**	**Income per Household**	**Income per Household / 10,000**
1	Colorado	4673724	2,474,508	3,260,286	1.22702881	$ 50,652.00	$ 5.07
2	Missouri	5787885	3,081,156	3,732,549	1.177235726	$ 41,974.00	$ 4.20
3	Louisiana	4495670	2,002,682	3,258,336	1.170241143	$ 36,729.00	$ 3.67
4	Texas	22843999	10,945,498	15,620,248	1.162920117	$ 42,139.00	$ 4.21
5	Arkansas	2772152	1,313,238	1,781,266	1.116282224	$ 34,999.00	$ 3.50
6	New Mexico	1916331	909,041	1,170,436	1.085134562	$ 37,492.00	$ 3.75
7	Oklahoma	3535926	1,635,403	2,187,424	1.081138859	$ 37,063.00	$ 3.71
8	Kansas	2741665	1,284,666	1,666,340	1.076355426	$ 42,920.00	$ 4.29

Correlation Coefficient - 0.6155259

Websites used:

http://www.census.gov/hhes/www/income/income98.html

http://www.fcc.gov/Bureaus/Common_Carrier/Reports/FCC-State_Link/IAD/trend801.pdf

		Year - 2005	
	State	**Tele - Accessibility**	**Income per Household / 10000**
1	Colorado	1.22702	5.07
2	Missouri	1.17724	4.20
3	Louisiana	1.17024	3.67
4	Texas	1.16292	4.21
5	Arkansas	1.11628	3.50
6	New Mexico	1.08513	3.75
7	Oklahoma	1.08114	3.71
8	Kansas	1.07635	4.29

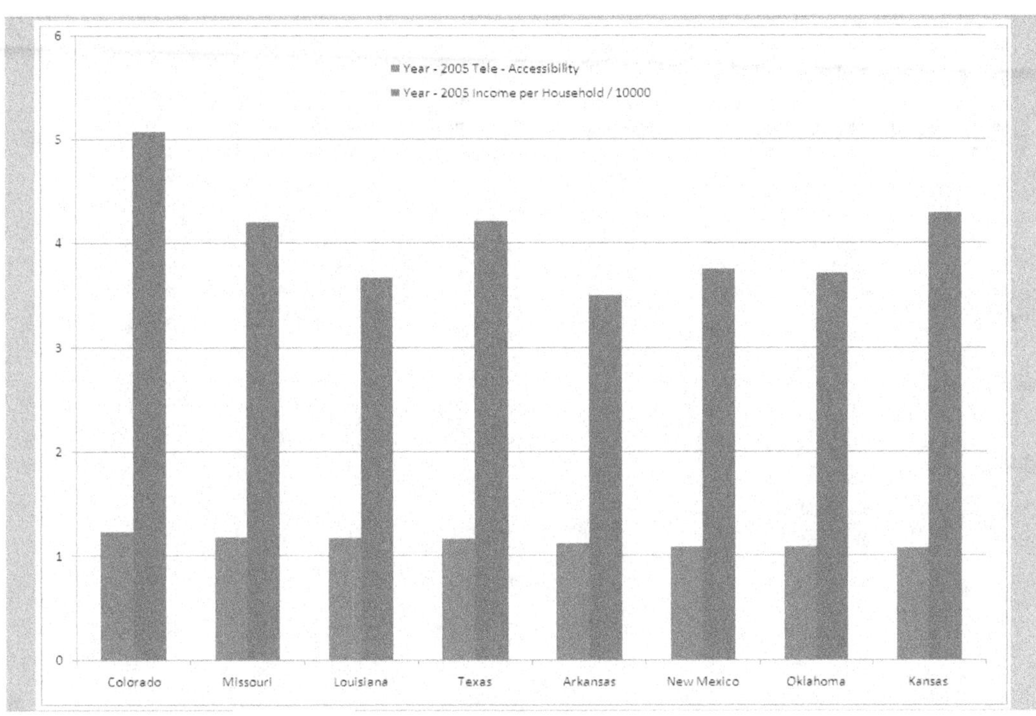
Year - 2005 Tele - Accessibility
Year - 2005 Income per Household / 10000
6
5
4
3
2
1
0
Colorado
Missouri
Louisiana
Texas
Arkansas
New Mexico
Oklahoma
Kansas

	Year - 2006						
	State	**Population**	**Number of Fixed Lines**	**Number of Mobile Lines**	**Tele - Accessibility (Fixed + Mobile lines /Population)**	**Income per Household**	**Income per Household / 10,000**
1	Louisiana	4243288	1,904,437	3,492,358	1.271842731	$ 37,740.00	$ 3.77
2	Missouri	5837639	2,927,211	4,322,458	1.241883748	$ 43,310.00	$ 4.33
3	Colorado	4766248	2,301,366	3,608,209	1.23987988	$ 52,275.00	$ 5.23
4	Texas	23407629	10,308,842	17,822,230	1.20179075	$ 43,546.00	$ 4.35
5	Kansas	2755817	1,191,789	2,046,542	1.175089275	$ 44,345.00	$ 4.43
6	Arkansas	2809111	1,246,108	2,044,217	1.17130473	$ 35,961.00	$ 3.60
7	New Mexico	1942302	872,062	1,333,210	1.135390892	$ 38,847.00	$ 3.88
8	Oklahoma	3577536	1,535,987	2,479,877	1.122522317	$ 38,191.00	$ 3.82

Correlation Coefficient - 0.3897679

Websites used:

http://www.census.gov/hhes/www/income/income98.html
http://www.fcc.gov/Bureaus/Common_Carrier/Reports/FCC-State_Link/IAD/trend801.pdf

	State	Year - 2006 Tele - Accessibility	Income per Household / 10000
1	Louisiana	1.27184	3.77
2	Missouri	1.24188	4.33
3	Colorado	1.23987	5.23
4	Texas	1.20179	4.35
5	Kansas	1.17509	4.43
6	Arkansas	1.17130	3.60
7	New Mexico	1.13539	3.88
8	Oklahoma	1.12252	3.82

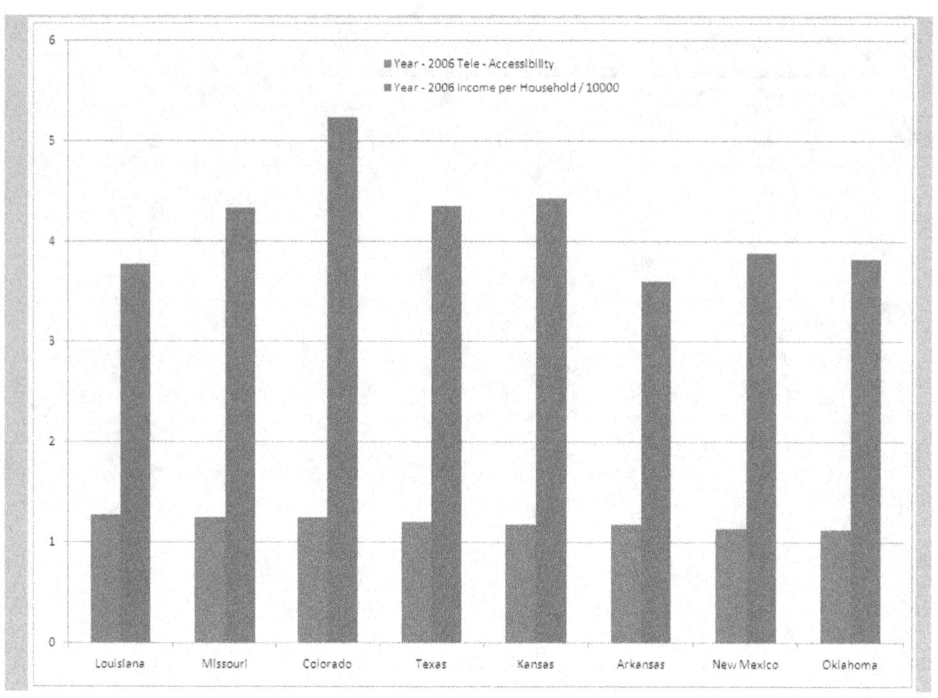
Year - 2006 Tele - Accessibility
Year - 2006 Income per Household / 10000
6
5
4
3
2
1
0
Louisiana
Missouri
Colorado
Texas
Kansas
Arkansas
New Mexico
Oklahoma

	State	Population	Number of Fixed Lines	Number of Mobile Lines	Tele - Accessibility (Fixed + Mobile lines /Population)	Income per Household	Income per Household / 10,000
				Years - 1996 - 2006			
1996	Arkansas	2504858	1,288,457	N/A	0.51438325	$ 27,471.00	$ 2.75
1997	Arkansas	2524007	1,368,534	N/A	0.542206896	$ 27,471.00	$ 2.75
1998	Arkansas	2538202	1,422,174	N/A	0.560307651	$ 27,471.00	$ 2.75
1999	Arkansas	2551373	1,501,281	719,919	0.870590071	$ 28,398.00	$ 2.84
2000	Arkansas	2,673,400	1,733,035	743,928	0.926521658	$ 30,293.00	$ 3.03
2001	Arkansas	2,690,254	1,509,333	970,127	0.921645317	$ 31,798.00	$ 3.18
2002	Arkansas	2,703,310	1,401,702	1,156,345	0.946264764	$ 32,423.00	$ 3.24
2003	Arkansas	2720006	1,415,060	1,296,901	0.997042286	$ 33,259.00	$ 3.33
2004	Arkansas	2742898	1,371,860	1,458,673	1.031949784	$ 33,131.00	$ 3.31
2005	Arkansas	2772152	1,313,238	1,781,266	1.116282224	$ 34,999.00	$ 3.50
2006	Arkansas	2809111	1,246,108	2,044,217	1.17130473	$ 35,961.00	$ 3.60

Correlation Coefficie 0.931307

Note:
In the years 1996-98 no reporting requirements were placed upon the cellular industry at that time period, thus limited information is available.

Websites used:

http://www.census.gov/hhes/www/income/income98.html
http://www.fcc.gov/Bureaus/Common_Carrier/Reports/FCC-State_Link/IAD/trend801.pdf

		Arkansas: 1996 - 2006	
Years	**State**	**Tele - Accessibility**	**Income per Household / 10000**
1996	Arkansas	0.51438	2.75
1997	Arkansas	0.54220	2.75
1998	Arkansas	0.56030	2.75
1999	Arkansas	0.87059	2.84
2000	Arkansas	0.92652	3.03
2001	Arkansas	0.92165	3.18
2002	Arkansas	0.94626	3.24
2003	Arkansas	0.99704	3.33
2004	Arkansas	1.03195	3.31
2005	Arkansas	1.11628	3.50
2006	Arkansas	1.17130	3.60

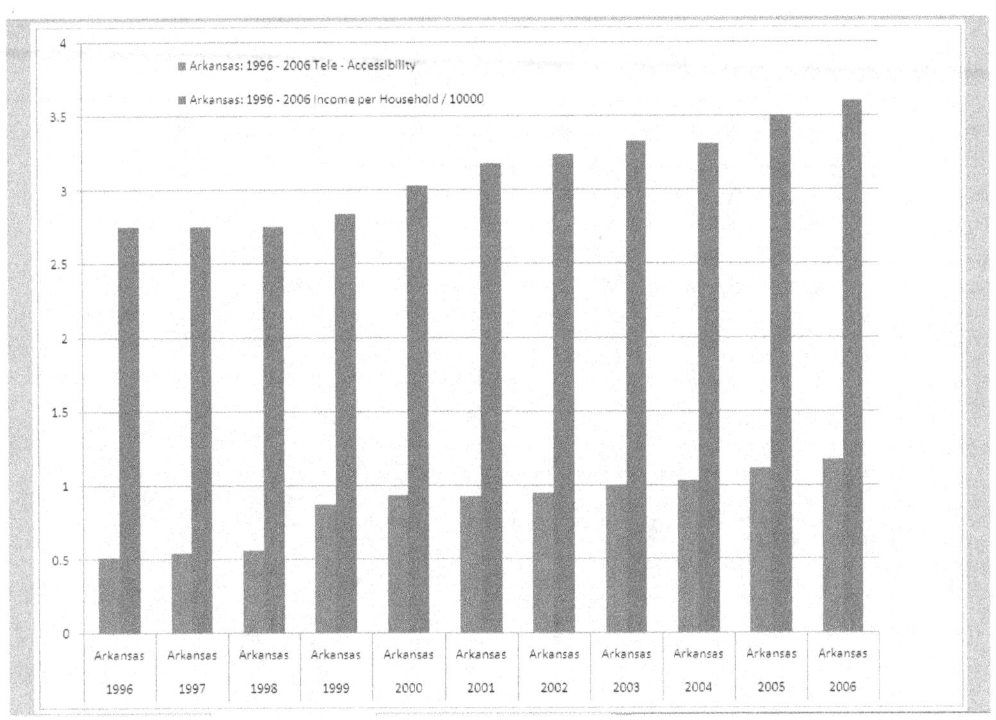
Arkansas: 1996 - 2006 Tele - Accessibility
Arkansas: 1996 - 2006 Income per Household / 10000
4
3.5
3
2.5
2
1.5
1
0.5
0
Arkansas 1996
Arkansas 1997
Arkansas 1998
Arkansas 1999
Arkansas 2000
Arkansas 2001
Arkansas 2002
Arkansas 2003
Arkansas 2004
Arkansas 2005
Arkansas 2006

	State	Population	Number of Fixed Lines	Number of Mobile Lines	Tele - Accessibility (Fixed + Mobile lines /Population)	Income per Household	Income per Household / 10,000
			Years - 1996 - 2006				
1996	Colorado	3812716	2,381,182	N/A	0.624536944	44,349.0	$ 4.43
1997	Colorado	3891293	2,643,505	N/A	0.679338462	44,349.0	$ 4.43
1998	Colorado	3968967	2,756,829	N/A	0.6945961	44,349.0	$ 4.43
1999	Colorado	4056133	2,864,170	1,552,718	1.088940624	46,950.0	$ 4.70
2000	Colorado	4,301,261	3,120,903	1,856,075	1.157097419	48,506.0	$ 4.85
2001	Colorado	4433997	2,948,466	2,145,816	1.148914174	50,053.0	$ 5.01
2002	Colorado	4507762	3,124,180	2,358,748	1.21633041	49,617.0	$ 4.96
2003	Colorado	4555212	2,706,855	2,554,731	1.155069402	50,224.0	$ 5.02
2004	Colorado	4609264	2,606,817	2,808,195	1.174810555	42,635.0	$ 4.26
2005	Colorado	4673724	2,474,508	3,260,286	1.22702881	50,652.0	$ 5.07
2006	Colorado	4766248	2,301,366	3,608,209	1.23987988	52,275.0	$ 5.23

Correlation Coefficient - 0.695697

Note:
In the years 1996-98 no reporting requirements were placed upon the cellular industry at that time period, thus limited information is available.

Websites used:

http://www.census.gov/hhes/www/income/income98.html
http://www.fcc.gov/Bureaus/Common_Carrier/Reports/FCC-State_Link/IAD/trend801.pdf

Colorado: 1996 - 2006

Years	State	Tele - Accessibility	Income per Household / 10000
1996	Colorado	0.62445	4.43
1997	Colorado	0.67934	4.43
1998	Colorado	0.69459	4.43
1999	Colorado	1.08894	4.70
2000	Colorado	1.15709	4.85
2001	Colorado	1.14891	5.01
2002	Colorado	1.21633	4.96
2003	Colorado	1.15507	5.02
2004	Colorado	1.17481	4.26
2005	Colorado	1.22703	5.07
2006	Colorado	1.23987	5.23

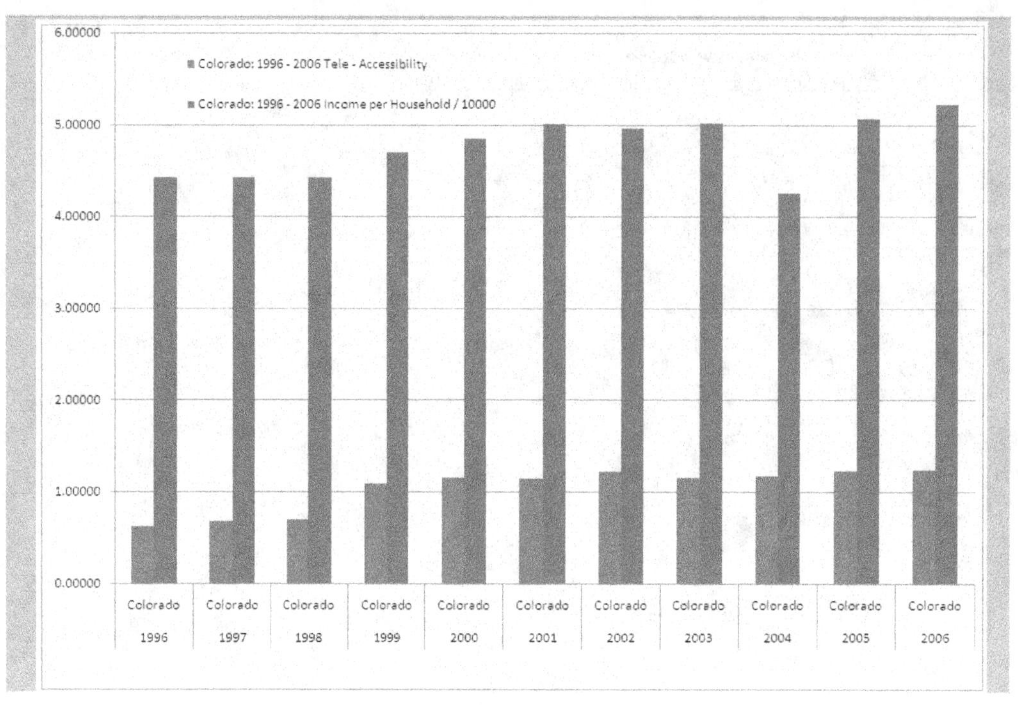
6.00000
5.00000
4.00000
3.00000
2.00000
1.00000
0.00000
Colorado: 1996 - 2006 Tele - Accessibility
Colorado: 1996 - 2006 Income per Household / 10000
Colorado 1996
Colorado 1997
Colorado 1998
Colorado 1999
Colorado 2000
Colorado 2001
Colorado 2002
Colorado 2003
Colorado 2004
Colorado 2005
Colorado 2006

	State	Population	Number of Fixed Lines	Number of Mobile Lines	Tele - Accessibility (Fixed + Mobile lines /Population)	Income per Household	Income per Household / 10,000
					Years - 1996 - 2006		
1996	Kansas	2598266	1,486,306	N/A	0.572037659	$ 35,867.00	$ 3.59
1997	Kansas	2616339	1,584,824	N/A	0.605741076	$ 35,867.00	$ 3.59
1998	Kansas	2638667	1,649,694	N/A	0.625199769	$ 35,867.00	$ 3.59
1999	Kansas	2654052	1,720,106	669,472	0.90035086	$ 37,618.00	$ 3.76
2000	Kansas	2,688,418	1,740,944	801,293	0.945625643	$ 37,705.00	$ 3.77
2001	Kansas	2700979	1,666,630	956,050	0.971010882	$ 41,097.00	$ 4.11
2002	Kansas	2712383	1,494,363	1,117,277	0.962858121	$ 42,523.00	$ 4.25
2003	Kansas	2721824	1,484,063	1,261,242	1.008626935	$ 43,622.00	$ 4.36
2004	Kansas	2730828	1,380,166	1,454,087	1.037873129	$ 37,952.00	$ 3.80
2005	Kansas	2741665	1,284,666	1,666,340	1.076355426	$ 42,920.00	$ 4.29
2006	Kansas	2755817	1,191,789	2,046,542	1.175089275	$ 44,345.00	$ 4.43

Correlation Coefficient - 0.823731

Note:
In the years 1996-98 no reporting requirements were placed upon the cellular industry at that time period, thus limited information is available.

Websites used:

http://www.census.gov/hhes/www/income/income98.html
http://www.fcc.gov/Bureaus/Common_Carrier/Reports/FCC-State_Link/IAD/trend801.pdf

		Kansas: 1996 - 2006	
Years	**State**	**Tele - Accessibility**	**Income per Household / 10000**
1996	Kansas	0.57204	3.59
1997	Kansas	0.60574	3.59
1998	Kansas	0.62519	3.59
1999	Kansas	0.90035	3.76
2000	Kansas	0.94563	3.77
2001	Kansas	0.97101	4.11
2002	Kansas	0.96286	4.25
2003	Kansas	1.00863	4.36
2004	Kansas	1.03787	3.80
2005	Kansas	1.07636	4.29
2006	Kansas	1.17509	4.43

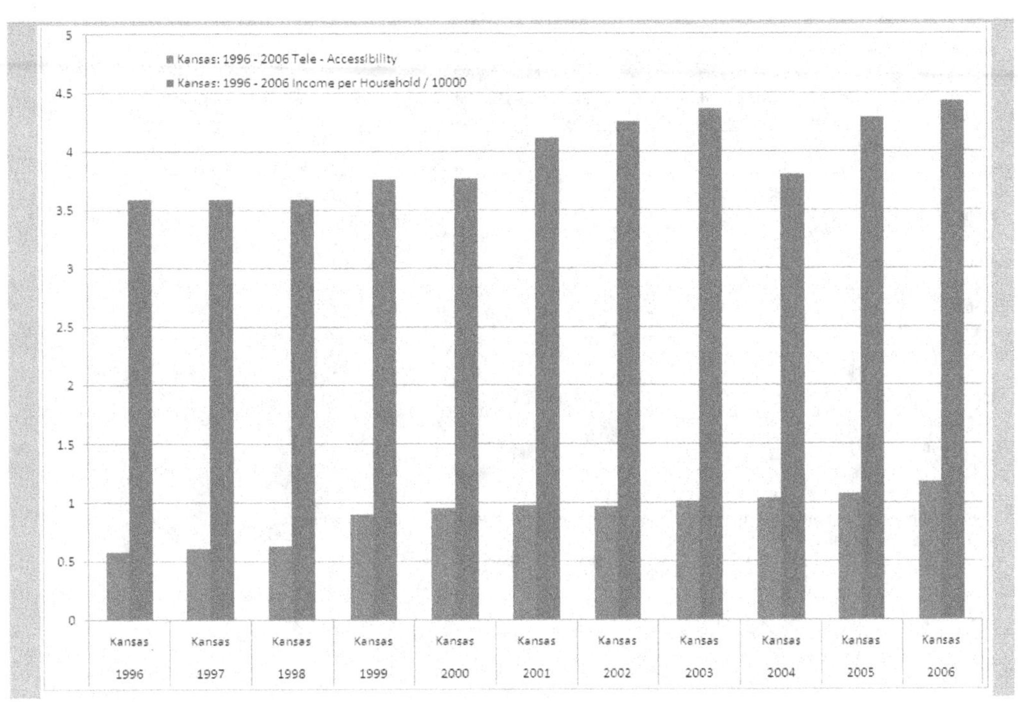

Kansas: 1996 - 2006 Tele - Accessibility
Kansas: 1996 - 2006 Income per Household / 10000
5
4.5
4
3.5
3
2.5
2
1.5
1
0.5
0
Kansas 1996
Kansas 1997
Kansas 1998
Kansas 1999
Kansas 2000
Kansas 2001
Kansas 2002
Kansas 2003
Kansas 2004
Kansas 2005
Kansas 2006

	State	Population	Number of Fixed Lines	Number of Mobile Lines	Tele - Accessibility (Fixed + Mobile lines /Population)	Income per Household	Income per Household / 10,000
				Years - 1996 - 2006			
1996	Louisiana	4338763	2,265,803	N/A	0.52222327	$ 32,317.00	$ 3.23
1997	Louisiana	4351390	2,435,338	N/A	0.559668979	$ 32,317.00	$ 3.23
1998	Louisiana	4362758	2,529,434	N/A	0.579778663	$ 32,317.00	$ 3.23
1999	Louisiana	4372035	2,585,779	1,227,106	0.872107611	$ 33,218.00	$ 3.32
2000	Louisiana	4,468,976	2,796,882	1,306,457	0.918183271	$ 30,219.00	$ 3.02
2001	Louisiana	4460285	2,575,040	1,920,740	1.007958012	$ 33,194.00	$ 3.32
2002	Louisiana	4465490	2,542,272	2,190,613	1.059880327	$ 33,312.00	$ 3.33
2003	Louisiana	4473679	2,388,005	2,470,146	1.0859409	$ 34,307.00	$ 3.43
2004	Louisiana	4487966	2,268,720	2,834,716	1.137137848	$ 36,873.00	$ 3.69
2005	Louisiana	4495670	2,002,682	3,258,336	1.170241143	$ 36,729.00	$ 3.67
2006	Louisiana	4243288	1,904,437	3,492,358	1.271842731	$ 37,740.00	$ 3.77

Correlation Coefficient - 0.719176

Note:

In the years 1996-98 no reporting requirements were placed upon the cellular industry at that time period, thus limited information is available.

Websites used:

http://www.census.gov/hhes/www/income/income98.html
http://www.fcc.gov/Bureaus/Common_Carrier/Reports/FCC-State_Link/IAD/trend801.pdf

Lousiana: 1996 - 2006			
Years	**State**	**Tele - Accessibility**	**Income per Household / 10000**
1996	Louisiana	0.52222	3.23
1997	Louisiana	0.55967	3.23
1998	Louisiana	0.57978	3.23
1999	Louisiana	0.87211	3.32
2000	Louisiana	0.91818	3.02
2001	Louisiana	1.00796	3.32
2002	Louisiana	1.05988	3.33
2003	Louisiana	1.08594	3.43
2004	Louisiana	1.13714	3.69
2005	Louisiana	1.17024	3.67
2006	Louisiana	1.27184	3.77

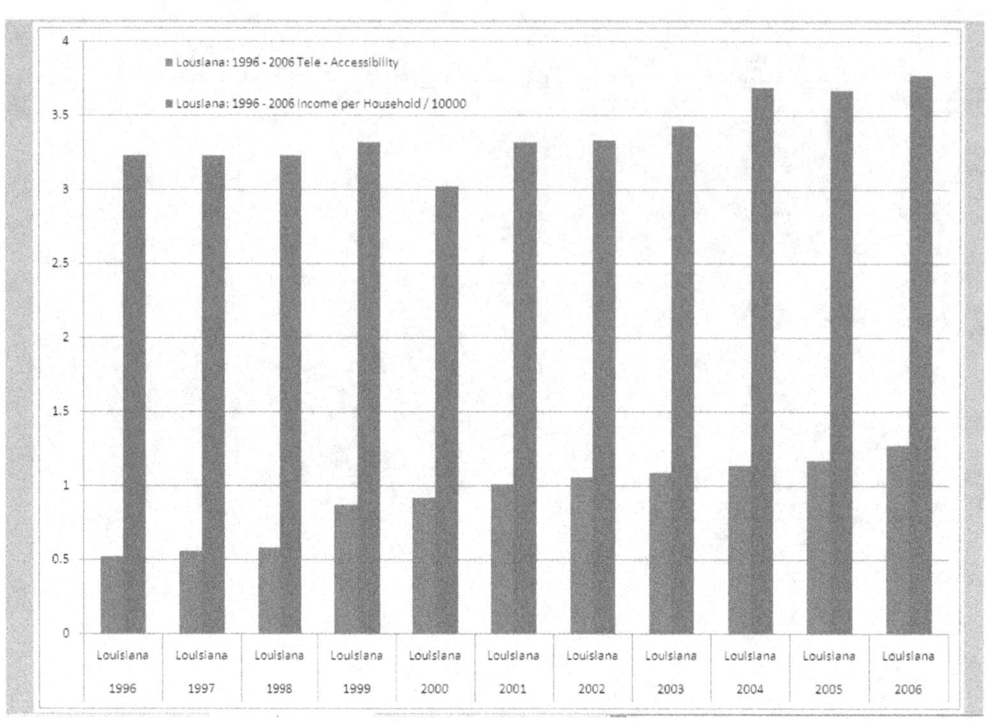
Lousiana: 1996 - 2006 Tele - Accessibility
Lousiana: 1996 - 2006 Income per Household / 10000
4
3.5
3
2.5
2
1.5
1
0.5
0
Louisiana 1996
Louisiana 1997
Louisiana 1998
Louisiana 1999
Louisiana 2000
Louisiana 2001
Louisiana 2002
Louisiana 2003
Louisiana 2004
Louisiana 2005
Louisiana 2006

					Years - 1996 - 2006			
	State	**Population**	**Number of Fixed Lines**	**Number of Mobile Lines**	**Tele - Accessibility (Fixed + Mobile lines /Population)**	**Income per Household**	**Income per Household / 10,000**	
1996	Missouri	5367888	3,064,182	N/A	0.570835681	$ 37,640.00	$	3.76
1997	Missouri	5407113	3,324,016	N/A	0.614748758	$ 37,640.00	$	3.76
1998	Missouri	5437562	3,450,562	N/A	0.634578879	$ 37,640.00	$	3.76
1999	Missouri	5468338	3,626,683	1,855,452	1.00252307	$ 40,166.00	$	4.02
2000	Missouri	5,595,211	3,688,948	1,767,411	0.975183778	$ 47,462.00	$	4.75
2001	Missouri	5641517	3,630,138	2,106,599	1.016878439	$ 43,884.00	$	4.39
2002	Missouri	5676209	3,482,767	2,289,831	1.016981228	$ 43,955.00	$	4.40
2003	Missouri	5705971	3,386,695	2,691,255	1.065191183	$ 43,492.00	$	4.35
2004	Missouri	5744753	3,247,190	3,109,167	1.106463063	$ 38,637.00	$	3.86
2005	Missouri	5787885	3,081,156	3,732,549	1.177235726	$ 41,974.00	$	4.20
2006	Missouri	5837639	2,927,211	4,322,458	1.241883748	$ 43,310.00	$	4.33

Correlation Coefficient - 0.6225211

Note:
In the years 1996-98 no reporting requirements were placed upon the cellular industry at that time period, thus limited information is available.

Websites used:

http://www.census.gov/hhes/www/income/income98.html
http://www.fcc.gov/Bureaus/Common_Carrier/Reports/FCC-State_Link/IAD/trend801.pdf

		Missouri: 1996 - 2006	
Years	**State**	**Tele - Accessibility**	**Income per Household / 10000**
1996	Missouri	0.57084	3.76
1997	Missouri	0.61475	3.76
1998	Missouri	0.63458	3.76
1999	Missouri	1.0025	4.02
2000	Missouri	0.97518	4.75
2001	Missouri	1.01688	4.39
2002	Missouri	1.01698	4.40
2003	Missouri	1.06519	4.35
2004	Missouri	1.10646	3.86
2005	Missouri	1.17724	4.20
2006	Missouri	1.24188	4.33

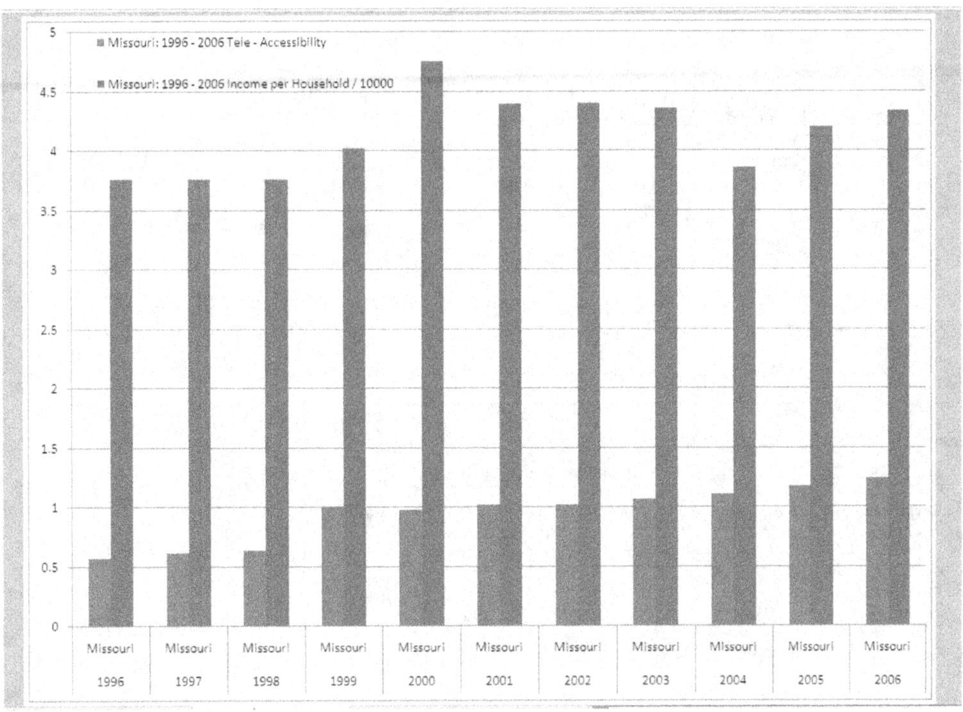
Missouri: 1996 - 2006 Tele - Accessibility
Missouri: 1996 - 2006 Income per Household / 10000
5
4.5
4
3.5
3
2.5
2
1.5
1
0.5
0
Missouri 1996
Missouri 1997
Missouri 1998
Missouri 1999
Missouri 2000
Missouri 2001
Missouri 2002
Missouri 2003
Missouri 2004
Missouri 2005
Missouri 2006

	State	Population	Number of Fixed Lines	Number of Mobile Lines	Tele - Accessibility (Fixed + Mobile lines /Population)	Income per Household	Income per Household / 10,000
					Years - 1996 - 2006		
1996	New Mexico	1706151	814,166	N/A	0.477194574	$ 29,386.00	$ 2.94
1997	New Mexico	1722939	901,359	N/A	0.523152009	$ 29,386.00	$ 2.94
1998	New Mexico	1733535	925,007	N/A	0.533595803	$ 29,386.00	$ 2.94
1999	New Mexico	1739844	954,496	363,827	0.757724831	$ 31,981.00	$ 3.20
2000	New Mexico	1,819,046	957,195	443,343	0.769929952	$ 35,254.00	$ 3.53
2001	New Mexico	1829032	1,003,993	660,849	0.910231204	$ 34,599.00	$ 3.46
2002	New Mexico	1850562	965,816	780,855	0.943859757	$ 35,251.00	$ 3.53
2003	New Mexico	1870113	967,109	859,408	0.97668804	$ 35,265.00	$ 3.53
2004	New Mexico	1892182	940,052	987,813	1.018858123	$ 35,040.00	$ 3.50
2005	New Mexico	1916331	909,041	1,170,436	1.085134562	$ 37,492.00	$ 3.75
2006	New Mexico	1942302	872,062	1,333,210	1.135390892	$ 38,847.00	$ 3.88

Correlation Coefficient - 0.9570754

Note:
In the years 1996-98 no reporting requirements were placed upon the cellular industry at that time period, thus limited information is available.

Websites used:

http://www.census.gov/hhes/www/income/income98.html
http://www.fcc.gov/Bureaus/Common_Carrier/Reports/FCC-State_Link/IAD/trend801.pdf

		New Mexico: 1996 - 2006	
Years	**State**	**Tele - Accessibility**	**Income per Household / 10000**
1996	New Mexico	0.47719	2.94
1997	New Mexico	0.52315	2.94
1998	New Mexico	0.53359	2.94
1999	New Mexico	0.75772	3.20
2000	New Mexico	0.76992	3.53
2001	New Mexico	0.910231	3.46
2002	New Mexico	0.94386	3.53
2003	New Mexico	0.97669	3.53
2004	New Mexico	1.01886	3.50
2005	New Mexico	1.08513	3.75
2006	New Mexico	1.13539	3.88

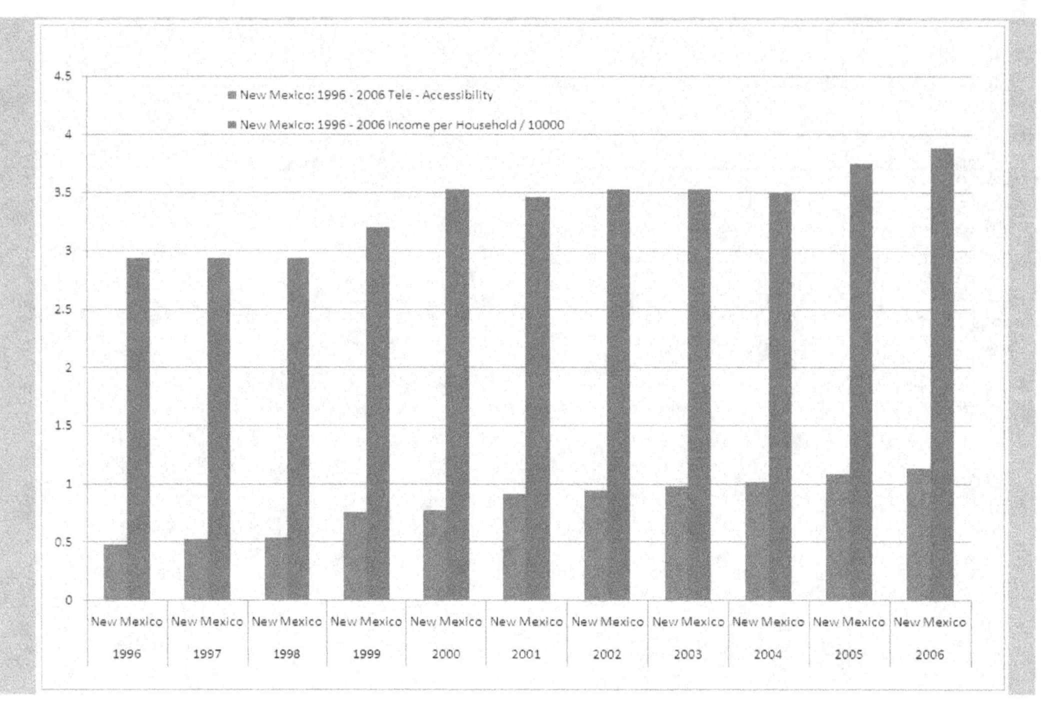

4.5
4
3.5
3
2.5
2
1.5
1
0.5
0
New Mexico: 1996 - 2006 Tele - Accessibility
New Mexico: 1996 - 2006 Income per Household / 10000
New Mexico 1996
New Mexico 1997
New Mexico 1998
New Mexico 1999
New Mexico 2000
New Mexico 2001
New Mexico 2002
New Mexico 2003
New Mexico 2004
New Mexico 2005
New Mexico 2006

	Years - 1996 - 2006						
	State	**Population**	**Number of Fixed Lines**	**Number of Mobile Lines**	**Tele - Accessibility (Fixed + Mobile lines /Population)**	**Income per Household**	**Income per Household / 10,000**
1996	Oklahoma	3289634	1,822,825	N/A	0.554111795	$ 31,357.00	$ 3.14
1997	Oklahoma	3314259	1,954,375	N/A	0.589686865	$ 31,357.00	$ 3.14
1998	Oklahoma	3339478	2,018,166	N/A	0.604335767	$ 31,357.00	$ 3.14
1999	Oklahoma	3358044	2,085,686	826,637	0.867267671	$ 33,311.00	$ 3.33
2000	Oklahoma	3,450,654	1,739,301	1,124,214	0.829847038	$ 32,445.00	$ 3.24
2001	Oklahoma	3464818	2,035,796	1,288,357	0.959401908	$ 34,554.00	$ 3.46
2002	Oklahoma	3485515	1,934,157	1,440,970	0.968329501	$ 35,500.00	$ 3.55
2003	Oklahoma	3499937	1,826,796	1,614,191	0.98315684	$ 36,733.00	$ 3.67
2004	Oklahoma	3516552	1,732,438	1,760,122	0.993177408	$ 34,503.00	$ 3.45
2005	Oklahoma	3535926	1,635,403	2,187,424	1.081138859	$ 37,063.00	$ 3.71
2006	Oklahoma	3577536	1,535,987	2,479,877	1.122522317	$ 38,191.00	$ 3.82

Correlation Coefficient - 0.9332328

Note:
In the years 1996-98 no reporting requirements were placed upon the cellular industry at that time period, thus limited information is available.

Websites used:

http://www.census.gov/hhes/www/income/income98.html
http://www.fcc.gov/Bureaus/Common_Carrier/Reports/FCC-State_Link/IAD/trend801.pdf

Years	State	Tele - Accessibility	Income per Household / 10000
		Oklahoma: 1996 - 2006	
1996	Oklahoma	0.55411	3.14
1997	Oklahoma	0.58969	3.14
1998	Oklahoma	0.60434	3.14
1999	Oklahoma	0.86727	3.33
2000	Oklahoma	0.82985	3.24
2001	Oklahoma	0.95940	3.46
2002	Oklahoma	0.96833	3.55
2003	Oklahoma	0.98316	3.67
2004	Oklahoma	0.99317	3.45
2005	Oklahoma	1.08113	3.71
2006	Oklahoma	1.12252	3.82

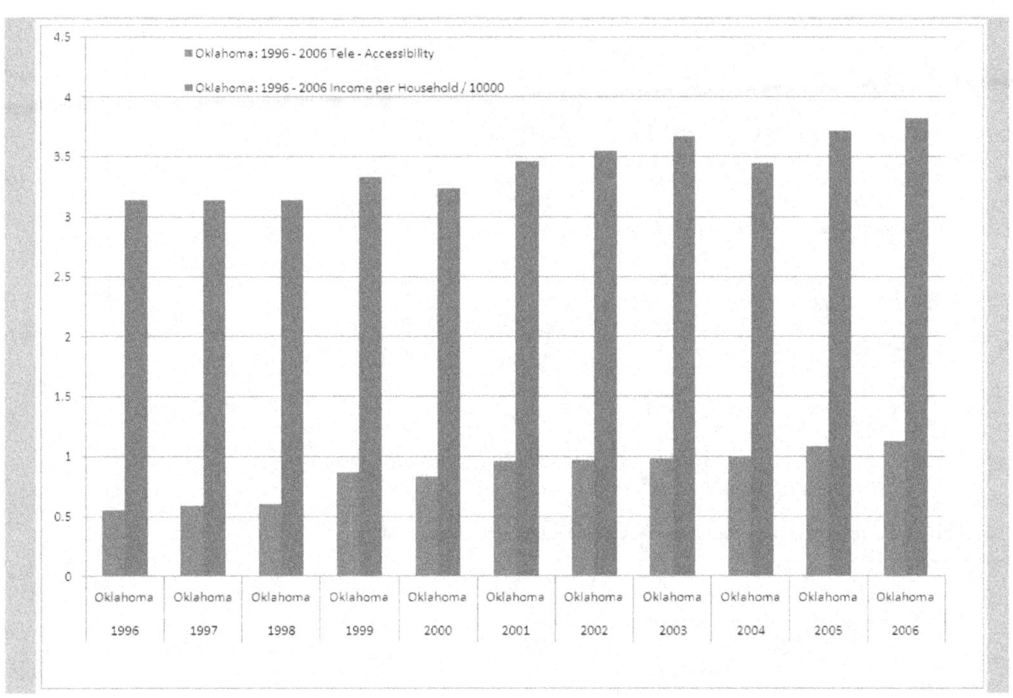
Oklahoma: 1996 - 2006 Tele - Accessibility
Oklahoma: 1996 - 2006 Income per Household / 10000
4.5
4
3.5
3
2.5
2
1.5
1
0.5
0
Oklahoma 1996
Oklahoma 1997
Oklahoma 1998
Oklahoma 1999
Oklahoma 2000
Oklahoma 2001
Oklahoma 2002
Oklahoma 2003
Oklahoma 2004
Oklahoma 2005
Oklahoma 2006

	State	Population	Number of Fixed Lines	Number of Mobile Lines	Tele - Accessibility (Fixed + Mobile lines /Population)	Income per Household	Income per Household / 10,000
			Years - 1996 - 2006				
1996	Texas	19006240	10,678,438	N/A	0.561838533	$ 35,254.00	$ 3.53
1997	Texas	19355427	12,006,252	N/A	0.620304166	$ 35,254.00	$ 3.53
1998	Texas	19712389	12,616,588	N/A	0.640033433	$ 35,254.00	$ 3.53
1999	Texas	20044141	13,174,403	5,792,453	0.946254369	$ 37,320.00	$ 3.73
2000	Texas	20,851,820	13,750,684	7,489,180	1.018609599	$ 39,842.00	$ 3.98
2001	Texas	21340494	13,192,061	9,156,187	1.047222618	$ 40,547.00	$ 4.05
2002	Texas	21730350	12,949,056	10,133,280	1.062216485	$ 40,659.00	$ 4.07
2003	Texas	22085973	12,039,565	11,327,700	1.058013835	$ 40,934.00	$ 4.09
2004	Texas	22454811	11,590,497	13,092,007	1.099207827	$ 38,200.00	$ 3.82
2005	Texas	22843999	10,945,498	15,620,248	1.162920117	$ 42,139.00	$ 4.21
2006	Texas	23407629	10,308,842	17,822,230	1.20179075	$ 43,546.00	$ 4.35

Correlation Coefficient - 0.91767359

Note:
In the years 1996-98 no reporting requirements were placed upon the cellular industry at that time period, thus limited information is available.

Websites used:

http://www.census.gov/hhes/www/income/income98.html
http://www.fcc.gov/Bureaus/Common_Carrier/Reports/FCC-State_Link/IAD/trend801.pdf

Years	State	Tele - Accessibility	Income per Household / 10000
		Texas: 1996 - 2006	
1996	Texas	0.46184	3.53
1997	Texas	0.62030	3.53
1998	Texas	0.64003	3.53
1999	Texas	0.94625	3.73
2000	Texas	1.01861	3.98
2001	Texas	1.04722	4.05
2002	Texas	1.06222	4.07
2003	Texas	1.05801	4.09
2004	Texas	1.09921	3.82
2005	Texas	1.16292	4.21
2006	Texas	1.20179	4.35

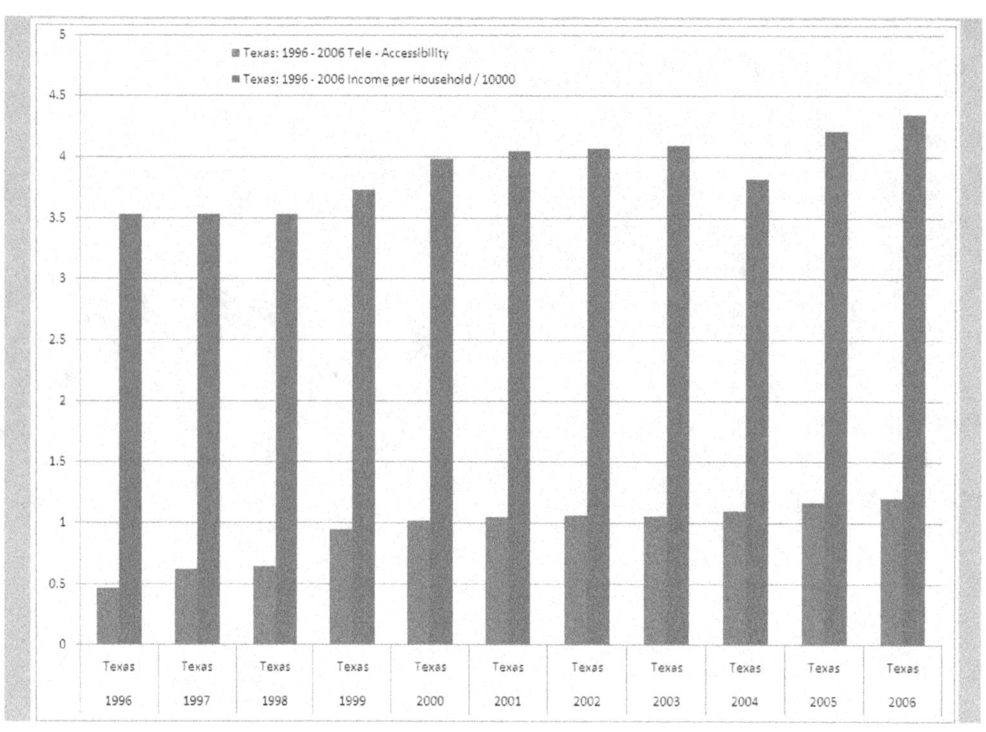
Texas: 1996 - 2006 Tele - Accessibility
Texas: 1996 - 2006 Income per Household / 10000
5
4.5
4
3.5
3
2.5
2
1.5
1
0.5
0
Texas 1996
Texas 1997
Texas 1998
Texas 1999
Texas 2000
Texas 2001
Texas 2002
Texas 2003
Texas 2004
Texas 2005
Texas 2006

Contact Information

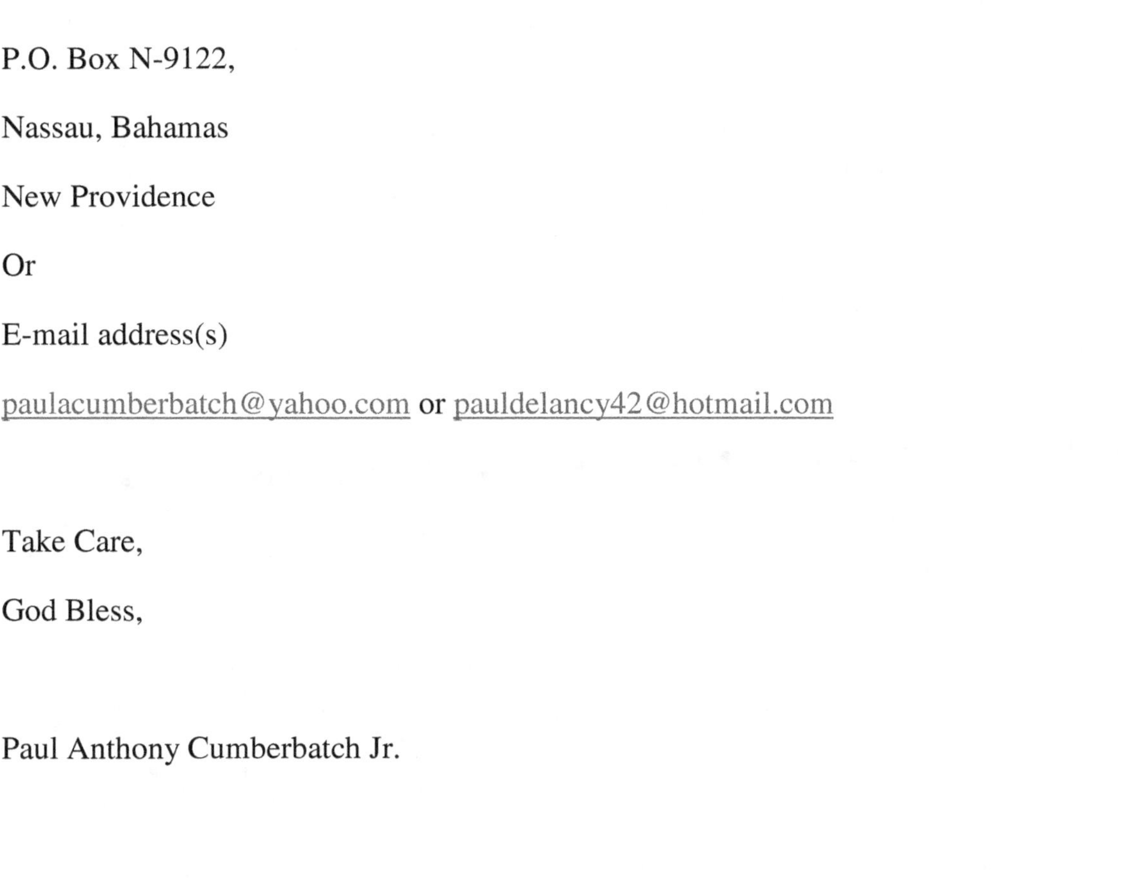

If you would like to contact us to ask questions, provide comments, or obtain information about possibly consulting or speaking engagements, please write a letter to the following postal or e-mailing address.

P.O. Box N-9122,

Nassau, Bahamas

New Providence

Or

E-mail address(s)

paulacumberbatch@yahoo.com or pauldelancy42@hotmail.com

Take Care,

God Bless,

Paul Anthony Cumberbatch Jr.

www.ingramcontent.com/pod-product-compliance
Lightning Source LLC
Chambersburg PA
CBHW081213170526
45165CB00009B/2812

9781452837802